GROUNDWORK GUIDES

Series Editor
Jane Springer

GROUNDWORK GUIDES

Oil

James Laxer

Groundwood Books
House of Anansi Press

Toronto Berkeley

Groundwood Books / House of Anansi Press
110 Spadina Avenue, Suite 801, Toronto, Ontario M5V 2K4
or c/o Publishers Group West
1700 Fourth Street, Berkeley, CA 94710

We acknowledge for their financial support of our publishing program the Canada Council for the Arts, the Government of Canada through the Book Publishing Industry Development Program (BPIDP) and the Ontario Arts Council.

ONTARIO ARTS COUNCIL
CONSEIL DES ARTS DE L'ONTARIO

Library and Archives Canada Cataloguing in Publication
Laxer, James
Oil / by James Laxer.
(Groundwork guides)
Includes bibliographical references and index.
ISBN-13: 978-0-88899-815-6 (bound).
ISBN-10: 0-88899-815-5 (bound).
ISBN-13: 978-0-88899-816-3 (pbk.)
ISBN-10: 0-88899-816-3 (pbk.)
1. Petroleum industry and trade — Political aspects. 2. Petroleum industry and trade — Economic aspects. 3. Petroleum reserves — Political aspects. 4. Energy consumption — Environmental aspects. 5. World politics — 21st century. I. Title. II. Series.
HD9560.5L39 2008   333.8'232   C2007.905780-2

Design by Michael Solomon
Printed and bound in Canada

Contents

To Robert

Acknowledgments

I am delighted to be involved again with a title in this important series of books, conceived by my good friend Patsy Aldana.

Thanks to Jane Springer, who did a fine job helping conceptualize this book and editing it. I am grateful to my literary agent, Jackie Kaiser, who offered encouragement and support.

My partner, Sandy, is always there with advice and companionship.

The team at Groundwood, Nan Froman, Michael Solomon and Leon Grek, deserve praise for the job they have done with this book and the entire series. And thanks to Deborah Viets, for her careful copyediting, and Lloyd Davis, for the index.

Chapter 1
The Hydrocarbon Age

In the early years of the twenty-first century, the world runs on petroleum. Take oil and natural gas out of the equation and transportation systems, home heating, agricultural and industrial production, and much of electric power generation would stall and grind to a halt. World oil production now totals about 75 million barrels a day (there are 35 gallons in a barrel). With only 5 percent of the world's population, the United States consumes 20 million barrels of oil a day, over a quarter of global consumption. Rounding out the top five oil-consuming countries are China (6.4 million barrels a day), Japan (5.8 million barrels), Russia (2.8 million barrels) and Germany (2.7 million barrels).

Oil is the fuel used to provide 90 percent of the energy consumed to propel automobiles, trains, airplanes and ships. About 40 percent of the energy consumed in the United States is provided by petroleum, oil and natural gas. Meanwhile the US produces less than half the oil it consumes, leaving the world's most powerful country increasingly dependent on imported oil. As China and

Hydrocarbons

Hydrocarbons are the chemical compounds (of hydrogen and
carbon atoms) from which all petroleum products are produced. Hydrocarbons are encountered in nature in liquid,
gaseous and solid forms.

Crude oil (the liquid form of petroleum) is used to produce
gasoline, diesel oil, heating oil and kerosene, and serves as
feedstock for the production of a wide range of chemical
products, plastics and medicines. It is also used to drive turbines for the production of electricity.

Natural gas (the gaseous form of petroleum) is used as a fuel to
heat homes and other buildings, to drive turbines for the
production of electricity, and as feedstock for the production of chemical products, plastics and medicines. It is used
to produce electricity as well. Natural gas can be liquefied
(to facilitate transportation or storage) and is used to provide fuel for vehicles, especially buses.

Petroleum comes in solid form as oil sands or oil shales.
Through an expensive process the oil (bitumen) can be separated from the sands or shales and the oil (synthetic
crude) can then be used in the ways crude oil is used.

Ethylene is produced from crude oil or natural gas through a
process known as "steam cracking." Ethylene is used widely
in the production of polyethylene to produce plastics and
vinyl, and was used in the past as an anesthetic. (It has
since been replaced by more efficacious anesthetics.) From
ethylene and its derivatives come garbage bags, milk jugs,
piping, automotive parts and film, among other products.

India rapidly industrialize, the global demand for oil is rising and is projected to continue to do so.

Increasing global demand for petroleum sets alarm bells ringing for governments, industries, farmers, consumers and environmentalists. Can oil production rise to meet the higher levels of demand? Since there is a finite amount of petroleum in the world and we are quickly consuming it, how long will there be enough oil to keep our societies running? As the price of petroleum rises sharply due to higher demand and limits on supply, what effect will this have on the standard of living and the way of life of people in the advanced countries and in the developing world? Can new sources of energy replace petroleum as oil supplies run out? On top of all of this, there is the urgent environmental challenge. The consumption of oil and natural gas (both hydrocarbons), and of other carbons such as coal, releases greenhouse gases into the atmosphere and contributes to the evermore acute problem of global warming and climate change. Can the world's leaders reach agreements, along the lines of the Kyoto environmental accord (which the US opposes) and subsequent accords, to prevent emissions from the consumption of carbon-based fuels from threatening the planet?

Considering how dependent the world now is on petroleum consumption, it may come as a surprise to learn that in historical terms the large-scale use of oil is a recent phenomenon. The modern oil industry had its origins in Canada and the United States on the eve of the American Civil War. In 1858, the first oil well in North

America was drilled in Petrolia, Ontario, and the following year, an oil well drilled in Titusville, Pennsylvania, ushered in the petroleum age in the US. A decade prior to the drilling of these pioneer wells, Canadian geologist Dr. Abraham Gesner discovered the technique for refining kerosene from coal. A few years later a Pole, Ignacy Lukasiewicz, figured out how to distill kerosene from oil. That discovery quickly created a huge international market for kerosene.

Up until that time, the illuminant of choice had been whale oil. Before kerosene became readily available, a gigantic whaling industry operated in various parts of the world, including New England. The whaling industry's principal goal was to hunt the huge seagoing mammals who served as a source of oil to light lamps and to provide lighting on the streets of American towns and cities. The American whaling fleet comprised 735 ships in 1846. By the 1850s, the price of whale oil had reached an all-time high, selling in 1856 for $1.77 a gallon, a price which if translated into today's dollars would be twenty or thirty times the contemporary price of gasoline.[1] Within a few years, as kerosene replaced it, the price of whale oil plunged (to forty cents a gallon by 1895), and the whaling industry fell on hard times. Most whaling operations on the east coast of the US went out of business. The relentless law of supply and demand was at work. When a cheaper, superior product came on the market — the price of refined oil was under seven cents a gallon in 1895 — the older, more expensive product was driven out of the marketplace. (One effect of the rise of the petroleum industry is that it almost certainly saved many species of whales from extinction.)

Oil did not have a smooth start as an industry. In 1878, Henry Woodward, a Canadian, invented the electric lightbulb and sold the patent to Thomas Edison. As this new invention spread, the demand for kerosene dried up and the oil industry fell into a recession. In the mid-1880s, the industry was rescued, and this time the rescue was permanent. The internal combustion engine, which employed gasoline to power automobiles, was pioneered in Europe by Karl Benz and Wilhelm Daimler. In the first years of the twentieth century, the mass age of the automobile was ushered in, with the incorporation by Henry Ford of the Ford Motor Company in 1903. In 1908, Ford launched the Model T Ford, which sold initially for $980. Over the next seventeen years, the Model T — Ford bragged that you could buy it in any color you liked as long as it was black — sold more than 15 million cars, with its price at one point dipping as low as $280. The Ford assembly line, fully in place in the company's Highland Park, Michigan plant in 1914, turned out an automobile chassis in ninety-three minutes, a technique that made cars affordable to millions of Americans. What had been a plaything of the rich was becoming the new means of transportation for the masses. Automobiles revolutionized American cities and the American way of life, ensuring an ever-rising demand for oil, the black gold that became the indispensable fuel on which the modern world ran.

Petroleum is so much a part of our lives today that it

seems remarkable that its large-scale use began only a century and a half ago. It's not that human beings did not encounter oil before the 1850s. Indeed, oil wells were drilled in China as long ago as the fourth century. The oil was then burned to bring brine to a boil, evaporate it and leave behind the salt residue that was the desired product. In Baghdad, during the eighth century, petroleum was readily available in the region and was used to produce tar to pave the streets.

In the decade before the first oil wells were drilled in North America, wells were drilled near Baku — then a part of the Russian Empire and now the capital of the Azerbaijan Republic — by a Russian engineer, F. N. Semyenov. A Russian oil refinery was built in the region in 1861 and for a short time Baku produced about 90 percent of the world's oil.

It was in the United States, though, that the modern oil industry took off. Along with the technological breakthroughs that created a vast market for petroleum came a uniquely powerful group of companies that dominated the oil industry from its earliest days. The oil industry came of age in the US during the decades following the Civil War, at a time when giant corporations were springing into being to take advantage of the uniquely large national market. One of the first and most famous of these was Standard Oil, the creation of John D. Rockefeller, whose success made him the world's first billionaire. In 1882, Rockefeller incorporated the Standard Oil Company of New Jersey. The company was to become a mammoth enterprise that controlled much of the petroleum industry, not only in the United States but worldwide.

So powerful was Standard Oil that it became the target of the famous "trust busters" in the US during the first years of the twentieth century. These reformers set out to prevent companies like Rockefeller's from becoming monopolies that could destroy the operations of the free market. In May 1911, the US Supreme Court ruled that Standard Oil was a combination (a monopoly) that violated the Sherman Anti-Trust Act. The court ruling forced the division of the huge trust into thirty-eight separate companies, many of which were to go on to become major players in the global petroleum industry. The largest of these companies, Standard Oil of New Jersey, commonly called Jersey Standard, went on to build a veritable global empire that made the assets of the old Standard Oil look small. Under its present name, ExxonMobil, the company operates in more than a hundred countries. On its own and in conjunction with other companies, including state-owned enterprises in the major petroleum-producing countries, ExxonMobil remains a powerful force in the global oil industry. If the purpose of the Supreme Court decision of 1911 was to end the control of the industry by monopolistic corporations, it would have to be judged a failure.

Soon Jersey Standard was joined by other giant petroleum companies, some based in the US and others in Western Europe. By the 1920s, seven huge companies, the so-called seven sisters, had gained a dominant place in world petroleum. In addition to Jersey

Standard, there were four other American companies: Mobil, Gulf, Texaco and Standard of California (Socal). Rounding out the seven were two European companies: Royal Dutch Shell and Anglo-Iranian (now British Petroleum). These giants fought vicious competitive wars against each other, but they also came together to make deals to share markets and to divide the world between them into spheres of influence for the exploration of oil. The seven sisters created the classic relations of what economists call an oligopolistic industry (one overwhelmingly dominated by a few strong players). In 1928, top officials of three of the giant oil companies, Jersey Standard, Shell and Anglo-Iranian, held a meeting at Achnacarry Castle in Scotland where they reached an agreement to divide markets and oil fields on a global scale. Their goal was to eliminate price competition among themselves.

The golden age of the domination of world oil by the seven sisters lasted until the early 1970s. By that date, the United States was slipping as the world's largest producer of petroleum. Its major oil reserves had been discovered and developed. Other regions of the world, principally the Middle East, were becoming the crucial center on which global oil production came to depend. Even before that date, other oil-producing countries were taking steps to ensure a higher price for their oil and to win a higher share of the profits earned from oil, most of which had been going to the giant oil companies. In 1960, under the leadership of Venezuela, the governments of the world's major oil-exporting countries met to form a cartel (an organization operated by the sellers of a basic product) to win better terms for themselves. The initial purpose of the Organization of Petroleum Exporting Countries (OPEC) was to prevent further declines in the international price of oil (which had been falling against the price of other products during the 1950s). Headquartered in Vienna, OPEC did not make much headway during the first decade of its existence. But in the 1970s, conditions changed. The United States was becoming increasingly dependent on imported oil. The surplus supply of oil was disappearing, which meant that a cartel that played its cards cleverly could do well for itself.

As has so often been the case in recent decades, what dramatically altered the situation was a political-military crisis in the Middle East. In the autumn of 1973, war broke out between Israel and its Arab neighbors. The war provoked a decision by the major Arab oil-producing countries to cut back on their petroleum production and to stop selling oil to the US and other countries deemed to be pro-Israel. The idea was that these members of OPEC would immediately cut their production by 25 percent to be followed by further cuts of 5 percent per month until Israel withdrew from the territory it had occupied since the Six-Day War of 1967. There were many peculiar aspects to this boycott of sales to the US, which need not detain us here. What did happen, though, was that the global price of oil shot up dramatically between December 1973 and mid-1974, from about $4 a barrel to $11 a barrel.

While the boycott failed in its stated political objectives, the OPEC countries did succeed, through this and other initiatives, in gaining a bigger share of the petroleum pie for themselves. In a number of cases, OPEC countries, including Saudi Arabia, the country with the largest conventional oil reserves in the world, moved to acquire partial or complete ownership of their oil industries. While this step weakened the control of the oil giants on their territories, the major oil companies retained enormous power. As a result of much higher global oil prices, the companies declared record-high profits in the years following 1973. They continued to ship, refine and retail a very large portion of the oil from the OPEC countries.

The new era of partnership between OPEC and the major oil companies lasted until the end of the 1970s. In fact, it was strengthened in 1979 when revolution in Iran resulted in the toppling of the Shah of Iran and the establishment of the new Islamic Republic under the leadership of the Ayatollah Khomeini. The resulting turmoil took Iran's oil off the world market for a time and the global price of petroleum doubled again. Two years later, however, OPEC's hold on the global supply of oil faltered. New supplies came on the market from the North Sea fields and OPEC members cheated on one another, producing more oil than their OPEC quotas allowed. The consequence was that the price of oil plummeted from about $30 a barrel to about $10 a barrel. For oil-producing regions such as Texas and Alberta, hard times were back. Unemployment soared and cities like Houston and Calgary felt the downturn. Relatively low oil prices prevailed through the 1980s and 1990s, but high prices returned with a vengeance in the new century. By the summer of 2006, the price of a barrel of oil soared to $70, and then fell back from that level in subsequent months only to climb to $98 a barrel in November 2007. While there were bound to be frequent fluctuations in the price in response to shifts in demand and political crises in volatile oil-producing regions, most experts predicted that the trend line would be toward still higher prices.

It is no exaggeration to assert that we have entered the crisis of the petroleum age. Just as a century and a half ago the rising price of whale oil and the pressure on whale species from overhunting created a predicament, rising demand and limited supply are at the heart of the global petroleum crisis. The petroleum crisis is by no means confined to the supply and demand of a vital commodity. It is inseparable from a rapidly emerging environmental problem of monumental proportions. To make matters worse, because so much of the world's most readily accessible petroleum is located in zones of military and political conflict, the quest for oil is intimately tied up with bloodshed and war.

In the next chapter, we will explore the basics of petroleum and the petroleum industry. In subsequent chapters we will scrutinize the economics and politics of oil with a detailed look at oil in the Middle East, in Russia and the Caspian Sea region, and in the Western Hemisphere. We will investigate the environmental costs of excessive petroleum use and the viability of alternative sources of energy. The book concludes with a discussion of the approaches humanity can take to grapple successfully with the global petroleum crisis.

Chapter 2
Petroleum and the Petroleum Industry

Most geologists agree that the earth's petroleum formed over millions of years through the pressures brought to bear on the remains of small animals buried beneath successive layers of mud and shale rock. The process is similar to that which produced coal, except that coal was derived from plants rather than animals. In the case of petroleum, under enormous pressure that generated heat, the remains of organisms were converted into fatty liquids and solids. In this natural furnace of the earth, over eons of time, the makeup of these substances was transformed into the molecular form found in oil. The presence of bacteria played an essential role in removing oxygen and converting the cooking material into hydrocarbons (liquid carbons). Once in liquid form, the immense pressures that created the furnace forced the hydrocarbons out of shale into more porous rock formations — limestone, dolomite or sandstone — which were located in close proximity to the shale where the petroleum was formed.

The world's great oil reservoirs were established through the workings of the earth's tectonic processes, the continual shifting of land masses and continents, one consequence of which is that layers of rock can be tilted as tectonic plates grind against one another. Where uptilting has occurred in rock formations bearing oil, the oil has been pushed upward, often being sealed at the top by layers of shale, through which the oil cannot pass. In some cases, oil located near the surface seeps out and can be found in pools on the ground or in rivers and streams. Natural gas is formed through a similar process, but it tends to occur at depths of more than 7,620 meters (25,000 feet), where the pressures are even greater than those at which oil is created. Under these greater pressures, the biological mass that is the basic ingredient of petroleum is converted into natural gas.

Oil is also found in oil sands, or tar sands, as they are often called. In the form of what is known as bitumen, oil is located in a liquid or semiliquid state in limestone, sandstone or sand. Oil produced from oil sands requires an extremely expensive industrial process to extract the bitumen and then to separate the oil from the sand. Current oil sands technology necessitates the use of vast quantities of natural gas and water. In the process, enormous quantities of sand are dug up. All of this results in serious environmental damage. These issues are addressed in Chapter 5, in the discussion of the huge oil sands deposits in Alberta.

Petroleum can take gaseous, liquid or solid forms. In the case of oil, it is encountered in liquids of greater or lesser viscosity (thickness) and in a range of hues from jet black to nearly colorless. Petroleum can be refined for human use into various forms, including natural gas, gasoline, naphtha, kerosene, fuel and lubricating oils, paraffin wax and asphalt. Petroleum is also a valuable feedstock for the production of chemical products and medicines.

At first glance, petroleum is like a gift from the gods, an energy source that is transportable and useful in meeting the needs of an industrial civilization. No wonder it was seen as black gold. In the early days of drilling for oil, when a well came in and threw a great black shower into the air, the drillers stood in it, reveling and luxuriating as the valuable liquid poured over them.

Nectar of the gods perhaps, but the first crucial fact about petroleum is that it is a finite commodity formed over millions of years that is being consumed in a variety of human activities at a very rapid rate. Beginning in the mid-nineteenth century, a huge industry has grown up to explore for, extract, refine, ship and retail petroleum and petroleum products. Over time the techniques used to extract petroleum have developed considerably. A crucial and increasingly sophisticated aspect of the industry involves exploration for undiscovered petroleum reserves. Making use of their knowledge of the geological conditions in which petroleum is likely to occur and employing technological expertise, including mapping from satellites in earth orbit, exploration companies have avidly searched large parts of the earth's surface and the floors of seas and oceans to find petroleum. (These exploration companies operate as independent entities or as divisions of larger companies.)

The quest for petroleum by exploration companies and by geologists with an enhanced knowledge about where the substance may be lurking coexists with another pursuit, the increasingly anxious analysis of how much oil there is in the world and how long it will be available for human consumption.

In the middle years of the twentieth century, a remarkable American petroleum analyst, M. King Hubbert, developed a theory about how long petroleum reserves would last. His point of departure was the fact that new petroleum discoveries in the United States peaked in the early 1930s. Extrapolating from this and taking into account how long it would take to develop new reserves and how long American oil fields would continue to yield petroleum, he concluded that American petroleum production would peak in the early 1970s and would begin to decline thereafter. In fact, Hubbert turned out to be right about US oil production, which did peak in 1971 and has declined since then. Using variations on Hubbert's approach, analysts have made predictions about when the point of peak global petroleum production will occur and how rapidly production will decline from that point.

In the aftermath of the spectacular increases in global petroleum prices in 1973-74, there was a great deal of expert and public discussion about what was called "limits to growth." An influential group of intellectuals and political leaders came together in a body called the Club of Rome to warn governments and the general public about the fact that the earth's resources, including petroleum, were finite, and that economic planning for the future would have to take account of the capacity of the planet. This call for an approach to economics that took the environment centrally into account largely disappeared from view with the return to cheap oil after 1981 and the election of conservative leaders such as Margaret Thatcher in the United Kingdom in 1979 and Ronald Reagan in the United States in 1980. Both these leaders believed that the market system would steer the world through resource supply crises. Their theory was that if supplies of a resource such as oil became scarce, its price would rise and that this would promote the development of products that would use less of the resource — for instance, lighter and smaller vehicles — and would generate the scientific search for new sources of energy to replace oil. After all, that is what happened when petroleum replaced whale oil as a fuel in the nineteenth century.

This comparatively cheerful outlook has been seriously challenged once again in the early years of the twenty-first century, both in response to much higher petroleum prices and the dependence of the US and other advanced countries on increased imports of oil from regions of conflict and instability, chiefly the Middle East. Once again the issue of when world oil production will peak has returned with a vengeance. Many experts believe that the point of peak oil will be reached — if it has not already been reached — before 2010. (Some forecasts issued over the past fifteen years incorrectly predicted that 1989, 1990 or 1995-2000 would be the point when oil production would peak.) The investment company Goldman

Sachs picked 2007 as the year when global oil production would peak. Naturally, it takes a number of years after such a forecast date to determine whether the prediction has proven to be correct. If, for instance, the Goldman Sachs prediction is right, world oil production should begin a gradual decline after 2007. Other forecasts are more optimistic, putting the moment when peak oil production will be reached sometime in the next couple of decades or perhaps a little later.

As important as when peak oil production will be reached are the politically, militarily and economically salient facts about where the proven and projected reserves of petroleum are located. As the known international reserves of conventional oil reach their production peak, the world will become evermore dependent on the petroleum reserves located around the Persian Gulf. Six Persian Gulf countries — Saudi Arabia, Iraq, the United Arab Emirates (UAE), Kuwait, Iran and Qatar — sit on 64 percent of the world's known oil reserves. These six countries, located in one of the world's most politically volatile regions, possessed proven oil reserves estimated at 679 billion barrels in 2002. Other important sources (reserves in billions of barrels) included South and Central America with 98.6, Africa 77.4, the countries from the former Soviet Union 77.1, Asia 38.7, the United States 30.4, Canada and Mexico 19.5, and the North Sea countries 16.3. Estimates suggest that the world could be even more dependent on the Middle East as a source of petroleum in 2025 than it is today.[1]

The reserves listed here are called proven reserves.

These reserves exist in already discovered oil fields for which there are reliable estimates of their size. Beyond proven reserves, there are probable reserves, forecasts made by petroleum companies and geologists for how much additional petroleum is likely to be discovered based on our current expertise. Beyond both proven and probable reserves, there are unconventional sources of petroleum that come in the form of oil sands or oil shales. These sources are much more expensive to produce and their production leads to greater environmental damage than conventional sources. While little has been done to develop oil shales, found among other places in Colorado, oil sands production in Alberta is rapidly expanding. Some estimates suggest that Alberta's oil sands contain as much or even more retrievable oil than the conventional reserves of Saudi Arabia.

Especially in the early days of the petroleum industry, the techniques used to lift oil to the surface ended up leaving about two-thirds of the oil in a particular field still in the ground when the field was regarded as played out. These primary production methods were inefficient and wasteful. As the price of petroleum has increased, new and more expensive techniques to lift oil to the surface, known as secondary and tertiary methods, which include the injection of steam into a well, have resulted in the production of more of the oil from a field. Even with these techniques, however, a large percentage (as much as half) of the oil is never produced.

The Petroleum Industry

Since the mid-nineteenth century, one of the world's most powerful industries has developed to explore for, produce and deliver petroleum to the markets of the world.

John D. Rockefeller, who began his career as a book-keeper in his early twenties, was involved in the oil industry almost from its first days in the United States. Six years after the discovery of oil in Pennsylvania, the twenty-six-year-old Rockefeller bought a controlling interest in an oil refinery in Cleveland.[2] A cold, sharp-eyed and utterly unromantic character, Rockefeller learned early that the key to making big money in the oil business was not by being one of the roughnecks involved in bringing in new oil fields. Such men prospered when demand for oil was high and went broke when there was a glut on the market and prices crashed. Rockefeller calculated that by gaining control of the refining end of the business, and even more important, by securing a stranglehold over the transportation of oil to customers, he could beat his competitors, drive them out of business and develop his own company, Standard Oil. He first established Standard Oil as a joint stock venture in 1870. The company began with a capital base of $1 million, of which he owned just over a quarter.[3]

The technique that made Rockefeller successful and later notorious was that he played railroads off against one another, forcing them to grant him rebates from their published freight rates so that he could ship his oil to market at the lowest possible price. He even managed to force railroads to pay to Standard Oil rebates from the payments being made by competing oil companies to ship their oil. During periods when there was a glut of oil on the market, Rockefeller took advantage of his competitors' weakness to drive them out of business and acquire their assets at fire-sale prices. If these methods didn't work to break a competing firm, Rockefeller invaded the competitor's selling territory and undercut its prices until it collapsed.

In 1880, a legislative committee in New York State reported on the techniques used by Standard Oil:

> [It] owns and controls the pipelines of the producing regions that connect with the railroads. It controls both ends of these roads. It ships 95 percent of all the oil.... It dictates terms and rebates to the railroads. It has bought out and frozen out retailers all over the country. By means of the superior facilities for transportation which it thus possessed, it could overbid in the producing regions and undersell in the markets of the world. Thus it has... absorbed and monopolized this great traffic.[4]

Through these methods, Rockefeller constructed what came to be called a trust, a mammoth business organization that absorbed and drove out competitors to establish a monopoly or near monopoly in a key industrial sector. During this historical period trusts grew up in other sectors, such as Andrew Carnegie's United States Steel Corporation and J. P. Morgan's financial giant, the

John D. Rockefeller

John D. Rockefeller, the founder of Standard Oil, was one of the world's most ruthless businessmen, but he was also one of the first businessmen to become a major philanthropist. Born on July 8, 1839, in Richford, New York, the young Rockefeller moved with his family to a small town near Cleveland, Ohio. He attended high school in Cleveland and joined the Erie St. Baptist Church there. At the age of nineteen, he became a church deacon and at twenty-one he was named a trustee of the church. From the receipt of his first paycheck, Rockefeller donated 10 percent of his earnings, a tithe, to his church.

His strong attachment to the church did not prevent him from engaging in business practices that drew fierce criticism. In the early days of Standard Oil, most petroleum products were shipped to market by rail. The 1870s was a decade of intense competition between railroads, whose profitability depended on the volume of traffic they won. Taking advantage of this, Rockefeller used his position as the largest shipper of petroleum products to force railroad companies to grant him steep rebates on the rates he paid. In addition, he managed to compel railroads to pay him a rebate on the rates paid by his competitors to ship their oil. Thus he not only increased his profits by paying freight rates well below the published schedule of the railroads, he profited from the volume of oil shipped by his competitors. On top of these methods, Rockefeller engaged in what is called predatory pricing. To undercut other oil companies in their key markets, Standard Oil sold its products at extremely low prices. The goal, which often met with success, was to drive a competitor to the edge of financial ruin and to force it to sell out to Rockefeller's firm.

In 1902, John D. Rockefeller summarized his philosophy of life and business as follows: "The American beauty rose can be produced in the splendour and fragrance which bring cheer to its beholder only by sacrificing the early buds which grow up around it. This is not an evil tendency in business. It is merely the working out of a law of nature and a law of God."[5] The statement is an example of an outlook among businessmen of the time that is called Social Darwinism. Derived from Charles Darwin's theory of the evolution of species, thinkers in the late nineteenth and early twentieth centuries developed the idea that just as there is a struggle for survival among species, there is also a natural struggle for survival and dominance within society. Rockefeller was expressing the view that it is natural and godly for businessmen to fight for dominance and that many businesses must perish so that one among them can achieve great success.

Ohio senator Marcus Hanna, a contemporary, said of Rockefeller that he was "money mad, money mad, sane in every other respect but money mad."[6]

By 1902, John D. Rockefeller's fortune was worth about $200 million. By the time of his death in 1937, his net worth was estimated to be $1.4 billion. He was not only the world's first billionaire but, in relative terms, the wealthiest man who ever lived. His fortune, at the time of his death, constituted a higher proportion of the national wealth of the United States than the fortune of Bill Gates, the founder of Microsoft, and the world's richest man today.

The extent of Rockefeller's wealth was exceptional and so too was his career as a philanthropist. In 1884, he provided a major endowment for a college in Atlanta, Georgia, for black women. The institution was later named Spelman College in honor of Rockefeller's in-laws, who were strongly committed to the abolition of slavery before the US Civil War. Rockefeller's donation of $80 million to a small Baptist college in Chicago was crucial in launching the University of Chicago as a major center of learning by the beginning of the twentieth century. In 1901, he launched the Rockefeller Institute for Medical Research in New York; in 1965, the institute changed its name to Rockefeller University. In 1913, he established the Rockefeller Foundation, giving it $250 million to carry out work in medical training, public health and the arts.

Ida M. Tarbell, a crusading muckraker (the term used to describe the journalists who exposed the business practices of the so-called robber barons of the era), was not favorably impressed by Rockefeller's fortune. In *The History of the Standard Oil Company*, published in 1904, she drew the following conclusion about how society ought to judge Rockefeller and others like him: "When the business man who fights to secure special privileges, to crowd his competitor off the track by other than fair competitive methods, receives the same summary disdainful ostracism by his fellows that the doctor or lawyer who is 'unprofessional,' the athlete who abuses the rules, receives, we shall have gone a long way toward making commerce a fit pursuit for our young men."

House of Morgan. Fearful that the trusts were destroying free enterprise in the United States by replacing competition with combination, a political movement grew up to oppose the trusts' power. The culmination of this effort was the 1911 US Supreme Court decision that Standard Oil was a trust acting in violation of antitrust legislation and that the company had to be broken up into thirty-eight separate companies.

After 1911, the oil business took on a new structure with the successors of Standard Oil — Standard's off-spring as they have been called — going on to establish giant business empires of their own.

First among the giants was Standard Oil of New Jersey. Jersey Standard was the remnant of the broken-up Standard Oil trust. It had acted as the holding company that had managed all the rest. Even after the breakup, Jersey Standard continued to purchase oil on a large scale from the other Standard companies and it served as a supplier of capital to many of them, assisting them with the financing needed for their exploration and development activities.[7] The empire Jersey Standard built around the world, as Esso and later Exxon, became much larger than Standard Oil had been when it had been disassembled in 1911. At its zenith, before many oil-producing countries nationalized parts of their oil industries, Jersey Standard and its subsidiaries operated seventy refineries in thirty-seven countries. The company controlled reserves of just under 50 billion barrels of petroleum. At the beginning of the 1970s, the company's international production totaled 6 million barrels of oil a day, one-tenth of global production at the time.

The second among the major companies that were to constitute the seven sisters, a descendant of Standard Oil, was the Standard Oil Company of New York, commonly known from its telegraph address as Socony. This company started out after the breakup of Standard with no crude oil of its own. In the mid-1920s, it acquired a Texas company rich in crude by the name of Magnolia. In 1931, Socony merged with Vacuum, an oil company that specialized in producing lubricants. After the merger, the company name was changed to Socony-Mobil and later just to Mobil. Mobil was the smallest of the seven sisters.[8]

Third on the list of the majors was Standard Oil of California or Socal, a company created out of an unsuccessful struggle by California oil producers to remain independent of Rockefeller. In the 1890s, however, Rockefeller acquired the company that was to become Socal and kept it as part of his empire until the breakup in 1911. Once Socal was on its own after 1911, it specialized in the production of oil, and by 1919 it accounted for 20 percent of American oil production, making it at the time the largest single producer in the country.

These three offspring of the original Standard Oil, Jersey Standard, Mobil and Socal, continued to have many members on their boards who were members of all three companies, directors who dated back to the old Standard Oil days. John D. Rockefeller remained the principal shareholder of all three companies' boards. Critics often accused the three companies of acting in concert with one another, citing the fact that they sold their oil at the same price and under the same Standard name. While the managements of the three companies vehemently denied they were colluding, the companies did make deals to act together in many of their foreign operations.[9]

The fourth of the seven sisters was also an American company, Gulf Oil, and it rose in Texas, a state where antitrust legislation actually worked to limit the power of Standard Oil. What gave the new oil giant its start was a vast petroleum discovery made near the coast of Texas at Spindletop in 1901. The discovery was financed by the powerful Mellon family in Pittsburgh, founders of the Mellon bank. Anthony Lucas, an engineer who had served in the Austrian navy, oversaw the drilling that brought in the biggest gusher yet recorded, a stream of black oil that shot into the air twice as high as the drilling rig. Following a period of vicious infighting among the owners and managers of the new company, which took its name from the Gulf of Mexico, Gulf emerged as a highly productive company, producing oil in the southwest and selling it in the east.[10]

Another Texas company, Texaco, was the fifth of the sisters. Texaco also had its start from the rush of speculators to cash in on the great new discovery of oil at Spindletop. The company was launched by Joseph Cullinan from Pennsylvania, who began his oil business career working for Standard Oil. When he moved to Texas, he continued to enjoy secret financial backing from Standard. With only $50,000, he set up the Texas Fuel Company at Spindletop. Half of this sum came from a syndicate run by a former Texas governor and the other half came from a New York financier with ties to the Leather Trust. The company changed its name, first to the Texas Company and then to Texaco. It succeeded in finding more oil in Texas and in setting up a nation-wide marketing organization so it could compete against the cut-throat tactics of Standard Oil. In 1913, Texaco built a thirteen-story headquarters in Houston, which had become the financial center of the Texas oil industry. As had been the case with other oil companies, bitter struggles followed between the Texans at the production end of the business and the New Yorkers who organized finance and marketing. The easterners won, driving Cullinan out and bringing in an easterner who was a graduate of MIT, Elgood Lufkin, as the new company president in 1913.[11]

Well before the end of the nineteenth century, John D. Rockefeller and Standard Oil were determined to use the methods that had won dominance in the vast American market in the rest of the world. Marcus Samuel was the son of a successful businessman from the east end of London who had been an importer of fashionable boxes from Asia made of shells. Taking over from his father, Samuel first went into the coal business and then decided that the future lay with oil. His source of oil was Russia, which had opened the way for foreign companies to explore for petroleum in the Caucasus beginning in 1873. To market his oil in East Asia, in conjunction with his business partners, Samuel built storage tanks near the markets he sought in the Far East. He then ordered the construction of a fleet of oil tankers, built specially to meet the requirements for vessels allowed to sail through the Suez Canal. This master stroke enabled the new venture to ship Russian oil through the canal en route to Asian markets. Each of the tankers was named after a shell. There were the *Murex*, the *Conch*, the *Clam* and many others. Resisting an offer from Rockefeller to buy him out, Samuel established the Shell Transport and Trading Company in 1897, with its headquarters in London.

Another company that managed to brave the competitive wars against Standard Oil was a firm based in the Netherlands, Royal Dutch. The company was launched on the basis of oil discovered at Sumatra in the East Indies. Although smaller than Shell to begin with, the managers of Royal Dutch fought a shrewd and ultimately successful battle against their British rival. In 1906, Shell was forced to enter into a merger with the Dutch firm. Royal Dutch came out the stronger, with a 60 percent share in the new oil giant, Royal Dutch Shell, the sixth of the seven sisters.[12]

The seventh sister, also a British firm, was first named Anglo-Persian, then Anglo-Iranian and finally British Petroleum. It was established both for business and for British imperial reasons. Unlike the other six giants, each of them privately owned, this company would end up owned by the British government. The rise of what ultimately became BP was intimately connected with the British navy during a period of increasing tension with Germany, which was constructing a High Seas Fleet to challenge the supremacy of the Royal Navy. Until the end of the nineteenth century, the Royal Navy ran on coal and maintained coaling stations at strategic locations on the continents of the world as well as on lonely midocean islands. A central aspect of the struggle to keep the Royal Navy supreme against Germany was to upgrade the navy's ships, to build new ones and to retire those that were obsolete. Critical to this was the switch from coal to oil as the fuel of choice for Britain's warships. Admiral John Fisher, First Sea Lord during the years of upgrading the Royal Navy, strongly advocated the switch to oil. Winston Churchill, appointed to the cabinet position of First Lord of the Admiralty in 1911, was seized with the need to find a secure source of oil for the navy.

The real founder of the company that would become BP was William Knox D'Arcy, an Englishman who had made a fortune in an Australian gold rush. In 1901, the year of the Texas discovery at Spindletop, he heard about a French geologist's conjecture that there were great oil finds to be made in Persia (Iran). D'Arcy dispatched two representatives to Teheran who managed to make a deal with the grand vizier to grant them a concession to explore for oil on a territory nearly twice the size of Texas. The concession was handed over for £20,000 in cash, 20,000 £1 shares, and 16 percent of the net profits to come.

After several years of unsuccessful exploration, D'Arcy was forced to seek an injection of capital from Burmah Oil Company, a venture that had struck oil in Burma, part of the British Empire. With encouragement from the British government, Burmah put up capital and in 1908 a major oil discovery was made. In 1909, D'Arcy and Burmah Oil formed a new company, the Anglo-Persian Oil Company, with Burmah's chairman, Lord Strathcona, the financier behind the Canadian Pacific Railway, as chairman.

The British government kept a watchful eye over the fortunes of Anglo-Persian, regarding its venture in Persia as strategically important to the Royal Navy. The British sent a detachment of Indian troops to provide security for the drilling operations of the company. A 209-kilometer (130-mile) oil pipeline was built from the company's oilfields to Abadan, off the coast of Persia. From Abadan, the oil could be shipped by tanker to the markets of the world. This first great oil venture in the Middle East firmly established the new company as a major player.

Anglo-Iranian, under competitive pressure from Shell, carried out negotiations behind closed doors with the British government for a financial subsidy. Winston Churchill, in charge of the admiralty, decided that more was needed than a subsidy. After a commission reported back to him on the Persian oilfields, Churchill concluded that the British government needed a controlling share in the ownership of Anglo-Iranian. In 1913, Churchill addressed the House of Commons and made the case that "we must become the owners, or at any rate the controllers, at the source of at least a proportion of the natural oil which we require." The admiralty paid £2 million for a 51 percent stake in the company. Under the arrangement, it was undertaken that the company would always remain in British hands and that every director on its board would be a British subject. In addition, the British government was to appoint two members to the company's board. These members were to have a veto over decisions taken that had a bearing on foreign or military policy or on issues relating to oil contracts with the admiralty.[13]

In 1999, two of the seven sisters, Exxon and Mobil, merged to form a single giant company, ExxonMobil. In 1984, two more of the sisters, Socal (Chevron) and Gulf, merged under the name Chevron. In 2001, Chevron merged with Texaco, to become Chevron Texaco. The Texaco name has since been dropped — the company is

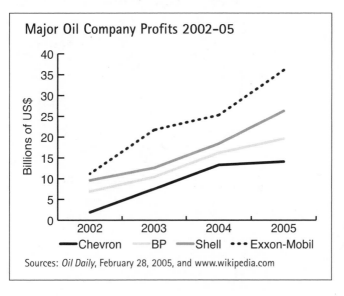

Major Oil Company Profits 2002–05

Sources: *Oil Daily*, February 28, 2005, and www.wikipedia.com

now known as Chevron. Nine decades after the US Supreme Court broke up Standard Oil, mergers were bringing large parts of its descendants together.

Each formed in its own particular way, with its own strengths and weaknesses, the seven sisters dominated the world oil industry for decades. While they continue to play a crucial role in the petroleum industry in the twenty-first century, they share power with other actors, the governments and state-owned companies of the oil-producing countries, the governments of the great powers, and new companies that have grown up to take a piece of the oil business.

In the next three chapters, we will focus on the economics, politics and security questions that surround the oil industry in three critical regions of the world: the Middle East, Russia and the Caspian Sea, and North America.

Chapter 3
Petroleum and Power Politics in the Middle East

Until the middle of the twentieth century, the United States dominated all other regions of the world in the volume of oil produced on its soil. As late as 1950, US oil fields still accounted for 52 percent of global petroleum production. By 1970, however, oil produced in the US amounted to only 22.8 percent of global production.

Its bountiful supply of oil was a crucial factor underlying the rise of the US as the world's greatest economic and military power. Over the course of the two world wars, access to petroleum grew ever more important in determining the military success or failure of the great powers. During World War II, the quest for secure sources of petroleum to underwrite their military power was crucial in shaping the war aims and military strategies of both Nazi Germany and Imperial Japan.

If the military adventures of Germany and Japan were much influenced by the need for petroleum, the United States was soon drawn into its own long-term drive to secure oil supplies for itself and its allies in both the Middle East and in the Western Hemisphere. With the emergence of Anglo-Persian, later BP, as a company controlled by the British government, the race of the oil companies into the Middle East was already underway. Even before World War II, American oil companies had begun an aggressive campaign to gain access to the oil reserves of the Middle East. In 1933, Socal (Standard Oil of California) negotiated a long-term right to explore for and produce oil in the easternmost province of Saudi Arabia, along the coast of the Persian Gulf. Socal focused on Saudi Arabia because its geology was similar to areas of Kuwait, Iraq and Persia where petroleum discoveries had already been made. In addition, while the oil-rich territories of these other Gulf states had already been parceled out to European companies, the promising regions of Saudi Arabia had not.[1]

The payment received by Saudi Arabia's ruler Ibn Saud was £35,000 sterling in gold and a share of future royalties. This was an exceedingly paltry sum of money to secure access to what was to be revealed as the greatest reservoir of cheap, easily accessible oil in the world. To push ahead with the development of the infrastructure needed to advance the project, Socal established a subsidiary, the California-Arabian Standard Oil Company (Casoc). Casoc (Texaco acquired a 50 percent ownership of the company in 1936) struck oil in Saudi Arabia in 1938. From 1939, when production began, to the end of World War II in 1945, output was small, with the total production from Saudi fields coming in at less than 1 percent of the production during the same period in the US.

Despite the relatively modest beginnings of oil production in Saudi Arabia, American geologists believed the potential for the future was enormous. Prompted by their rosy projections, the US government became increasingly interested in the implications of Saudi oil. Washington recognized the government of Ibn Saud in 1931, but it did not establish diplomatic relations with Saudi Arabia until 1939, and a full-time ambassador was only posted there in 1943. During the war, the Roosevelt administration came to realize how important Saudi oil could be in the future for the United States. Already concerned about the impending decline of domestic oil reserves, the administration wanted assured access to Saudi reserves. In February 1943, Roosevelt took the unusual step of extending Lend-Lease aid to Saudi Arabia even though the Lend-Lease Act was normally used to provide military equipment and other assistance to countries under attack "whose defense the president deems vital to the defense of the United States." Roosevelt was bending the rules for the Saudis, who had not been attacked by the Axis powers (Germany and Italy). In extending Lend-Lease aid to Saudi Arabia, Roosevelt declared that "the defense of Saudi Arabia is vital to the defense of the United States."[2]

So concerned were the Americans about the future control of Saudi oil that Secretary of the Interior Harold Ickes floated the idea of the United States government buying out Casoc's lease in the country. This would give Washington direct control of Saudi oil. In the words of Navy Under Secretary William C. Bullitt, who urged the scheme on the president, with this step "the estimated oil reserves of the United States would be approximately doubled."[3]

This plan never came to fruition because of opposition from Casoc's owners, from members of Congress who opposed the idea of any government ownership of the oil industry, and from the British, who still thought of Saudi Arabia as falling within the British sphere of influence.

While it was decided that the US government would not go the route of the British government when it acquired control of Anglo-Persian Oil, Washington continued to have a hands-on approach to Saudi oil. Two months before his death, during the last days of World War II, US President Franklin Roosevelt met with King Ibn Saud. The president was returning from his summit in Yalta with Stalin and Churchill. He flew to Egypt and then boarded the USS *Quincy*, an American warship anchored in the southern end of the Suez Canal. The president and the king met for more than five hours with only an interpreter present and no record was kept of what they said. It appears that at this meeting the Saudi monarch agreed to the establishment of an American air base at Dhahran.

A 1945 State Department memo summarized the view the US administration took toward Saudi Arabia at the end of the war and has taken ever since: "The oil resources of Saudi Arabia [are] among the greatest in the world" and they "must remain under American control for the dual purpose of supplementing and replacing our dwindling reserves, and of preventing this power potential from falling into unfriendly hands."[4]

The crucial role Saudi oil was to play in the world can be seen from the fact that between 1946 and 1976, Saudi oil production skyrocketed from a mere 60 million barrels a year to 3.1 billion barrels. In the mid-1970s, Saudi Arabia had become the world's third-largest oil producer, behind the United States, which was number one and the Soviet Union, which was number two. By 2002, the countries making up the former Soviet Union led the world with the production of 9.35 million barrels of oil a day, followed by Saudi Arabia with 8.68 million barrels a day and the US with 7.70 million barrels a day.[5]

In the early post-war period, as tensions increased between the United States and the Soviet Union, leading to the onset of the Cold War, the US developed a systematic approach to keeping the Soviets at bay. In the so-called Truman Doctrine, which President Harry S. Truman unveiled in 1947, it became American policy to resist Soviet aggression, whether that aggression took the form of the invasion of countries or the form of internal subversion. High on the list of objectives was to keep the crucial oil-producing Persian Gulf countries, including Saudi Arabia, safely under American control.

The first great struggle between the US and the Soviets over who was to control the oil-producing countries of the Middle East revolved around Iran. During World War II, the Soviet Union and Britain occupied Iran to prevent that country from falling into the hands of the Axis powers. The understanding was that both countries would pull their troops out within six months of the war's conclusion. After holding out past the deadline, under American pressure the Soviets did withdraw their troops in the spring of 1946.

Having pushed the Soviets out, the US was determined to keep them out. In October 1946, in a memo to the State Department, the Joint Chiefs of Staff stated that it was in the "strategic interest of the United States to keep Soviet influence and Soviet armed forces as far as possible from oil resources in Iran, Iraq, and the Near and Middle East."[6]

In Iran, the American mission changed from holding the Soviets at bay to intervention in the country's internal affairs. In 1951, a nationalist government under the leadership of Mohammed Mossadegh came to office in Iran. Just prior to Mossadegh's accession to the post of prime minister, the Iranian parliament voted to nationalize the Iranian petroleum industry and to take over the assets of the Anglo-Iranian Oil Company. The British government responded hastily to the takeover. Royal Navy ships were dispatched to the Persian Gulf to blockade Iran's ports in order to prevent the export of Iranian oil. When Dwight D. Eisenhower was sworn in as president of the United States in early 1953, his administration collaborated closely with the government of Winston Churchill in Britain to plot the overthrow of the Mossadegh government.

The scheme was overseen by US Secretary of State John Foster Dulles and his younger brother Allen, who was the director of the Central Intelligence Agency. In

April 1953, Allen Dulles budgeted $1 million to fund action "that would bring about the fall of Mossadegh." To oversee the plot, code-named Operation Ajax, the CIA sent Kermit Roosevelt Jr., the grandson of Theodore Roosevelt, to Teheran. It took some time for the scheme to bear fruit, but following clashes in the streets in the Iranian capital, in which close to 300 people died, Mossadegh was forced to resign. The forces of the Shah, funded by the CIA, were returned to power, and this first concerted effort in Iran to dispense with Western oil company control of their petroleum industry was halted.

The coup not only thwarted the cause of democracy in Iran, it fostered long-term anti-Americanism in that country. The role of the CIA in the coup has been acknowledged in the United States, although the American role was kept secret for many years. In March 2000, Madeleine Albright, then secretary of state in the Clinton administration, expressed regret at what had happened to the Mossadegh government: "The Eisenhower administration believed its actions were justified for strategic reasons. But the coup was clearly a setback for Iran's political development and it is easy to see now why many Iranians continue to resent this intervention by America."[7]

With the return of a pro-Western regime in Iran, the country's oil production rapidly increased over the remainder of the 1950s, making Iranian oil a key ingredient in the economic boom in the industrialized world during the period. With increasing petroleum production in the other Persian Gulf states of Saudi Arabia, Iraq and Kuwait, there was plenty of oil to fuel industrial expansion, to keep the price of oil down and to keep the seven sisters firmly in the driver's seat.

The next major upheaval in the Middle East did not directly concern the major petroleum-producing countries of the region, but it had important implications for them nonetheless. In the summer of 1956, the Egyptian government of Gamal Abdel Nasser nationalized the Suez Canal, which had been controlled by Europeans since 1869, the date it went into operation. In response to Nasser's move, the armed forces of Britain, France and Israel invaded the canal zone. However, both the United States and the Soviet Union opposed the invasion and the invaders were forced to withdraw. Nasser's stunning success against the traditional imperial powers made him the hero of much of the Arab world. He purchased weapons from the Soviet Union and engaged in an increasingly strong denunciation of the Western powers.

In response, the Eisenhower administration unveiled what came to be called the Eisenhower Doctrine in January 1957. Later embodied in legislation passed by the American Congress, the doctrine gave the president the authority to deploy US forces to defend pro-American Middle East regimes and supply these regimes with American weapons systems. Saudi Arabia, already the keystone in the American presence in the Persian Gulf, became a major beneficiary of American military aid. The American lease for its air base at Dhahran was extended. In return, the Saudis received the latest weapons, along with training to upgrade their army and air force and to establish a small navy. On top of that, the US supplied weapons and training to the Saudi Arabian National Guard (SANG), an internal security force whose job was to keep the authoritarian royal regime in power.[8]

Succeeding US administrations renewed the close alliance with Saudi Arabia and continued to supply the regime with advanced weapons systems. At the end of the 1960s, two vital changes affected the relationship of the United States with Saudi Arabia and the other Persian Gulf states. In 1968, the British government announced that it would withdraw its armed forces from its remaining bases "east of Suez." It was a key step in the winding up of what remained of the British Empire. The Americans, deeply embroiled in the Vietnam War at the time, had to decide whether to step into Britain's shoes and become the sole guardian of Western interests in this vital petroleum-producing region. In July 1969, the administration of President Richard Nixon came up with a doctrine of its own, the Nixon Doctrine. The emphasis in the doctrine, which was conceived mainly with Southeast Asia in mind, was that the United States would aid friendly countries resisting aggression with "military and economic resistance when requested." The American people were growing increasingly restive about the human and economic cost of the war in Vietnam and were highly skeptical about future missions involving large numbers of American troops. Nixon's idea was that the locals would do the fighting, but that they would be supplied with American weapons and training.

Both Saudi Arabia and Iran received billions of dollars' worth of the latest American military hardware. The pattern, not uncommon with such lavish provision of weapons, was to provide military advisers and technicians as well. In 1977, there were 6,250 Americans in these roles in Iran and 4,140 in Saudi Arabia.[9]

Despite American efforts to stabilize the Persian Gulf countries in the interests of American petroleum companies and the long-term relationship of these countries with the United States, political and economic developments led to crises. In 1960, under the leadership of Venezuela, the major oil-exporting countries decided to form an organization to improve their bargaining position vis-à-vis the major oil companies and the highly industrialized oil-importing countries. The Organization of Petroleum Exporting Countries (OPEC) began modestly, without much ability to influence the behavior of the seven sisters and the major oil-importing countries.

As early as June 1968, the members of OPEC adopted a set of objectives for their oil industries. These included: a preference for developing their petroleum through a company based in the producing country, increases in royalties and tax revenues for the producing countries, and the right of the government of the producing country to acquire a share of the ownership of its petroleum industry. Each of these goals pitted the OPEC countries against the oil companies, at least in their public rhetoric.

It wasn't until the early 1970s, however, that conditions changed and favored a much more substantial role for OPEC. By that date, the United States was becoming ever more dependent on imported oil. The major conventional oil reserves in the US were rapidly being depleted. Future oil developments in the United States were bound to involve more intensive (secondary and tertiary) recovery of oil from existing sources, the development of smaller oil fields, more drilling of offshore oil wells, and bringing oil into production from Alaskan fields. All these alternatives involved much higher costs.

The consequence of rising pressure for change within the OPEC countries, the geopolitics of the Middle East, and the needs of the United States as an oil-hungry superpower combined to produce what we can call the "oil price revolution."[10] Even before the war between Israel and its Arab neighbors during the autumn of 1973 — the event that triggered the oil price revolution — there were signs that a major price change was in the offing.

In 1950, net imports into the US amounted to less than 10 percent of the oil consumed by Americans. By 1970, net imports had grown to about one-third of American oil consumption. Over the course of these two decades, the American government wrestled with how to gradually increase oil imports, while maintaining the security of the national petroleum supply and looking out for the interests of both the seven sisters and national petroleum companies, whose chief operations were inside the United States.

By the early 1970s, the buyer's market for oil that had prevailed throughout the 1960s and 1970s was becoming a seller's market. US oil imports were increasing sharply and American domestic petroleum production actually declined in 1973 before the global crisis was unleashed in the last months of that year. As supply began to tighten, the OPEC countries managed to push up the price of oil from $1.80 a barrel to $3 a barrel between 1970 and 1973. In addition, the OPEC countries signed deals with the major oil companies that increased the royalties and taxes they received.

Many observers of the dramatic changes in the world petroleum industry during the early 1970s have assumed that the price increases were imposed by OPEC and opposed by the United States. That, however, is a simplistic analysis.

What actually happened proved more complex. The precarious competitive position of the US economy, because of the rise of competition from Western Europe and Japan during the Vietnam War and the decline of domestic oil reserves, made the idea of a higher global price for oil an attractive proposition to key members of the Nixon administration. Higher oil prices would close the gap between American oil prices and prices in the rest of the world, thus ending the price advantage then enjoyed by the Europeans and the Japanese. Higher prices would also increase the value of the remaining oil reserves in the United States, a very attractive proposition for domestic oil producers. And higher prices would act as an incentive to domestic oil producers to intensify exploration and production at home.

On the other hand, the alternative to a higher price for oil had its own considerable costs. A continuing low oil price would make it inevitable that the United States would have to increase imports from the Middle East and other parts of the world dramatically at a time when the US was already straining under a rising balance of payments deficit. If the price stayed low, it would be a disaster for the domestic oil industry.

For all these reasons, the Nixon administration had been won over to the need for a moderate increase in the world price of oil. It became common for members of the administration to talk publicly about the benefits of higher prices. For instance, a deputy interior secretary for energy made this statement in 1972: "Those who want industry to continue to provide adequate sources of energy but don't want any price increase which might provide capital for industry to do just that don't understand economics."[11]

A more important step came the same year when the Nixon administration sent James Akins, a state department official, to attend the Eighth Petroleum Congress of the League of Arab States in Algeria. At the meeting, Akins delivered a remarkable speech, considering who his audience was. He predicted that oil prices could be "expected to go up sharply due to lack of short-term alternatives to Arab oil."[12] While Akins's speech did not specifically advocate higher prices, it amounted to a green light to the Arab states, a clear signal that Washington would not oppose a price rise. A year later, Akins was appointed US ambassador to Saudi Arabia, an appointment that lent weight to his prediction that higher oil prices were coming. When a representative of the world's most powerful nation delivers such a clear signal to members of a cartel of oil-producing countries, dramatic consequences are likely to follow.

A week before the outbreak of war in the Middle East in October 1973, the OPEC countries met in Vienna and called for a petroleum price increase of between 80 and 100 percent. Then the war followed. Two weeks into the conflict, Israel found itself in serious difficulty. In response to a severe shortage of vital military equipment, the United States undertook an around-the-clock airlift to reequip its ally with needed materials. It was the restocking of Israel with weapons and equipment that provoked OPEC's members to announce their boycott of sales of petroleum to the United States and to increase the price of oil.

Once it was unleashed, the oil price revolution swept much further than the Nixon administration had wanted. In two jumps, the price vaulted upwards from about $3 a barrel to $11 a barrel. The oil price increase had the effect of pushing the world's leading industrial countries into a recession. The severe economic shocks — from higher transportation costs, higher costs for industry and agriculture and a blow to consumers in the form of steeper bills to heat their homes and fuel their cars — provoked many people in the industrial countries to adopt fantastic conspiracy theories to explain what had happened. In reality, the oil price revolution was not the consequence of a conspiracy. It resulted from a changing relationship among three key players: the OPEC countries, the major petroleum companies and the United States government. The three had complementary and contradictory interests and their shifting relationships brought about the dramatic increases in prices.

The oil price revolution ended the long era when the seven sisters and the governments of the United States and Britain were able to dominate the oil industry in the Middle East, treating the oil-producing countries as minor players. The Middle East countries gained much more power than they had previously had. In some cases, they acquired partial or full ownership of their oil industries, forcing the major oil companies to operate as the distributors of their product. With higher prices, enormous royalties and tax revenues flowed to the governments of Saudi Arabia, Iran, Iraq and the others, allowing them to build up the strength of their armed forces and to invest their oil wealth in other parts of the world.

As for the seven sisters, despite the fact that their world had become more complicated, they made profits undreamt of in the past. In January 1974, the major oil companies announced spectacular increases in their profits for 1973. Exxon Corporation (Jersey Standard) announced a profit of $2.44 billion, an increase of 59 percent over 1972. The new deal for the producing countries and the boycott had not hurt them — while their earnings on US operations were up only 16 percent in 1973, their operations on Eastern Hemisphere operations (mostly the Middle East) rose by a staggering 83 percent. The other six sisters all announced similarly huge increases in profits.

The new era in the history of the great oil-producing

countries did not remain stable for long. In 1979, the Iranian Revolution broke out and the regime of the shah, the close ally of the US, was overturned. The new power in Iran was the Ayatollah Khomeini who returned after a long exile in Paris to preside over the creation of an Islamic Republic. The virulent anti-Americanism of the new Iran was expressed most vehemently when Iranian students, with the blessing of the regime, invaded the US Embassy in Teheran on November 4, 1979, and seized the American staff, taking its members hostage. Fifty-two of the hostages remained in the hands of their captors until January 20, 1981, the day that Ronald Reagan was sworn in as president of the United States. The Iranian hostage crisis dealt a mortal blow to the administration of President Jimmy Carter. The crisis disrupted the flow of oil from Iran to the industrialized countries, leading to a tightening global oil supply and a further doubling of the price of crude oil. Between November 1978 and June 1979, the political turmoil in Iran resulted in a loss of production of between 2 million and 2.5 million barrels a day, with production almost halted at one point.

In September 1980, Iraq invaded Iran, setting off a bloody war that lasted eight years at a cost of a million lives. In this gruesome conflict, the US leaned toward the side of Saddam Hussein's Iraq, preferring a secular dictatorship to an Islamic Republic. While Iraq prevailed in the early stages of the conflict, with its larger population, Iran managed to mobilize and to fight the war to a stalemate. The Iran-Iraq war set the stage for Iraq's invasion of Kuwait in 1990.

The sharp rise in world oil prices as a consequence of the Iranian Revolution was followed a few years later by a steep decline in prices. Beginning in 1982, OPEC's efforts to set oil production quotas low enough to prevent a fall in prices was a failure. Because of increased oil production in Nigeria and by European countries in the North Sea, there was a glut of oil on the market. Saudi Arabia, with its vast reserves and productive capacity, tried to play the role in OPEC of the "swing producer," by cutting its own production to try to check the growth of the oil glut. The Saudis held their production of oil down to 2 million barrels a day. By the summer of 1985, the Saudi government concluded that the role of swing producer was costing too much. The Saudis decided to increase production to put pressure on the other OPEC countries to live up to their production quotas. In early 1986, Saudi Arabia increased its production of oil to 5 million barrels a day, provoking another fall in crude oil prices to below $10 a barrel by mid-1986.

Further efforts by OPEC members to tighten quotas and increase prices also failed, although the price of oil did increase following the Iraqi invasion of Kuwait and the Gulf War, which followed in 1991. Once the United States and its partners succeeded in pushing Iraq out of Kuwait, oil prices fell once again. In 1994, adjusting prices for inflation, the world price of oil dropped to its lowest level since the oil price revolution of 1973. During the latter half of the 1990s, on the strength of the enormous economic growth in East Asia, world consumption of oil increased by an additional 6.2 million barrels a day.

Oil prices climbed, but this recovery in prices ended with the onset of a severe economic crisis in Asia. When Asian economies resumed growth and as OPEC countries managed to reduce their output by 3 million barrels a day, the world oil price climbed to more than $25 a barrel.

New factors came into play that resulted first in a decline in oil prices after 2000 and then in a very sharp rise, driving prices to their highest levels ever. Prices first weakened as a result of a large increase in Russian oil production and a slowing of the US economy. OPEC countries tried to halt the decline by cutting their production quotas, but the terror attacks of September 11, 2001, provoked another sharp decline in the price of oil.

Since then, however, world oil prices have moved sharply upward. The Russians joined OPEC nations in cutting production in early 2002, and by March 2002 the price of world oil was back up to $25 a barrel. Political strife in Venezuela resulted in a reduction of oil production in this key South American country (see Chapter 5). Then came the US-led invasion of Iraq in March 2003, which drastically cut the production of Iraqi oil, just at the point when Venezuelan oil was coming back on stream. By 2004 and 2005, excess global petroleum capacity was rapidly disappearing. With Asian economies, led by China and India, importing evermore oil, the global price rose to $40 a barrel. By the spring of 2006, the price had shot up to $70 a barrel, and then up from there to the range of $80 a barrel, before it fell back again in September 2006 to about $60 a barrel. In a new surge, the price of oil reached $98 a barrel in November 2007.

As the price of oil reached unprecedented levels, a fierce debate erupted around the world about the future of industrial societies and the coming scarcity of petroleum. Not since the early 1970s had there been such a debate. While the debate in the 1970s and today turned on the geopolitics of the Middle East, the current debate also involves a much broader critical examination of US world policy.

The United States has continued the policy begun with Roosevelt's meeting with the Saudi king in 1945, regarding the petroleum reserves of the Middle East as a vital security issue for the United States. That explains why George Bush the elder was so insistent on assembling a very wide coalition of powers to drive Saddam Hussein out of Kuwait in the Gulf War of 1991. Similarly, the invasion of Iraq in 2003, undertaken by George W. Bush, had a great deal to do with the oil resources of the Persian Gulf. While the rationale for the American invasion, advanced by the Bush administration, was that Iraq possessed weapons of mass destruction (later admitted to have been a false claim), the subtext was the administration's desire to shore up its strategic hold on the Gulf.

In the years following the first Gulf War, the American policy of "keeping Saddam in his box" remained in place until the terror attacks on New York and Washington. By then George W. Bush was in office, and the key figures in his administration had a quite different strategic outlook on how to maintain American hegemony in the Persian Gulf from that of their predecessors. Previously, the US policy had been to anchor its position in the Gulf to its alliance with Saudi Arabia. George Bush the elder had held to this posture and had made the decision not to march on to Baghdad during the first Gulf War. After September 11, however, the White House became convinced that the US position in Saudi Arabia was shaky and that it needed to be buttressed. The radical idea that quickly gained ground among top decision-makers was that the American presence in the Persian Gulf would be strongly reinforced through an invasion and occupation of Iraq. Vice President Dick Cheney and Paul Wolfowitz, undersecretary of state, played a key role in convincing the administration that an occupied Iraq could be molded along American lines to become a model democracy in which Islamic fundamentalism would be countered by a society in which religion was a personal matter and not the basis for a theocracy. The Bush administration talked itself into the notion that an invading American army would be met as liberators by a grateful population, not only in the Shiite south and Kurdish north, but in the Sunni center as well. Iraq was to be America's tabula rasa in the Middle East, a blank slate on which a new beginning could be written. Once Iraq was liberated from Saddam's grip, the Americanized regime could easily be made to see the utility of the US maintaining permanent military bases in the country.

While the stated reason for the invasion of Iraq was to counter the threat of Saddam Hussein's weapons of mass destruction, the subtext was to oversee the vast oil reserves of the region and to ensure that they did not fall into hostile hands. It soon became clear, however, that the invasion of Iraq by the US and the "coalition of the willing" had created more problems for Washington than it had solved. As Iraq slid down the path toward civil war in the spring and summer of 2006, more and more mainstream voices in the United States were calling for the pullout of American troops.

With its 115 billion barrels of proven oil reserves, producible at very low prices relative to other sources, Iraqi oil could have been used to ease the strain in oil markets at a time of high demand. But one consequence of the chaos in Iraq was the falling level of production of its oil fields. Prior to Saddam's invasion of Kuwait in 1990, Iraq was producing 3.5 million barrels of oil a day. The Gulf War and the subsequent period of UN sanctions against Iraq were factors in driving Iraqi oil production down to 2.3 million barrels a day by the eve of the 2003 invasion. By December 2005, nearly three years after the American occupation of the country, Iraq's oil output was only 1.9 million barrels a day.

Not only was Iraq performing far below its potential as an oil producer, by the fall of 2006, US tension with Iran was threatening to disrupt that country's oil production as well. The crisis was over Iran's insistence on continuing to enrich uranium, ostensibly to provide fuel for nuclear power generation. The Bush administration, however, insisted that Iran's real purpose was to manufacture nuclear weapons, which would pose a threat to the Middle East and the US itself. While the United Nations

Security Council passed a resolution calling on Teheran to stop enriching uranium, permanent members of the council, Russia and China, were unwilling to vote for serious economic sanctions against Iran. With the Bush administration determined to halt Iran's nuclear program, tension continued to build. Some analysts feared that the United States would launch an aerial assault on Iran's nuclear facilities, possibly in conjunction with Israel.

Such an attack, were it to materialize, would certainly disrupt the flow of Iranian oil to world markets. Some observers have predicted that in the event of a US attack, Iran might attempt to shut the narrow waters of the Persian Gulf to the traffic of oil supertankers. If successful, this would dramatically impede the flow of oil to world markets, potentially leading to serious shortages and a surge in prices.

With the capture by the Democrats of both houses of the US Congress in the elections of November 2006, the Bush administration's strategy in the Persian Gulf lay in tatters. The American people had rejected the idea of fighting a long war to victory in Iraq no matter what the cost. Instead, top Republican and Democratic strategists were enlisted by the White House to find a way out of Iraq that would not result in too much of a loss of face for the United States. Under consideration was the idea of inviting both Syria and Iran into talks about Iraq's future. By the end of 2006, American and British occupying forces in Iraq had been reduced almost to the level of helpless spectators as civil war threatened to tear the country into three pieces — a Kurdish north, a Shiite south and a Sunni center.

Not least in doubt was the American grip on the Persian Gulf, a centerpiece of US policy for more than six decades. Washington had no intention of withdrawing from this crucial petroleum-producing region. Not out of the question, though, was the idea of moving American forces out of Iraq and into the secure base of Kuwait, from which both Iraq and the other countries of the Gulf could be warily monitored.

Chapter 4
Russian and Caspian Sea Petroleum and Its European Consumers

The collapse of the Soviet Union in 1991 ended a military threat to Western Europe that had existed from the end of World War II. The new chapter in relations between Russia and Europe was not free from considerable anxiety, however. The Russians have become essential providers of oil and natural gas to Europeans. The wealthy Europeans now keep a wary eye on Russia, a major oil supplier that has been going through a period of economic and societal chaos during the past couple of decades. A symbol of that chaos is the rickety Russian pipeline system that delivers oil and natural gas to European markets. Russian pipelines are so poorly maintained that they are riddled with leaks that have literally left lakes of petroleum along parts of their course.

The struggle of the world's great powers for petroleum for their own use and to control the access of other powers to petroleum is now focused on two regions of the world above all others. The first of these, of course, is the Persian Gulf. The second is the petroleum reserves in the area of the Caspian Sea. Three important petroleum producers are located in the Caspian Sea area. Russia, with 60 billion barrels of proven reserves at the end of 2002, is the largest of these, producing 7.7 million barrels a day, about 10.7 percent of global production, making it second in the world to Saudi Arabia in its oil production. In addition, Russia possesses the world's largest natural gas reserves. Next in importance is Kazakhstan, with proven reserves of 9 billion barrels and a daily production of just under 1 million barrels of oil daily. Third is Azerbaijan, with 7 billion barrels in proven reserves and an output of .31 million barrels daily.[1]

The breakup of the Soviet Union opened the way for an intense struggle involving the United States, Russia and China for access to, and control of, these vital petroleum reserves. In the wings are the Europeans, who are increasingly dependent on oil and natural gas from the region to fuel their automobiles, residences and industries.

For the Russians, struggling to sustain what was left of their position as a major power in the aftermath of the breakup of the Soviet Union, vast oil and natural gas reserves have become their trump card. In 2002, oil and natural gas constituted 55 percent of the value of Russia's exports and the petroleum business generated 40 percent of the country's government income. For the government of Russian president Vladimir Putin petroleum was the key to maintaining leverage over former Soviet republics that depended on Russian imports as well as over the European Union, which had to import most of its oil and natural gas. In addition, petroleum gave Russia clout in its broader global dealings with the

United States, China and Japan. In the generally gloomy setting of the Russian economy, energy has been the major bright spot. About 25 percent of the country's economy is now geared to the energy sector. The onset of higher petroleum prices in recent years has been a tonic for the Russian economy and state.

For the Putin government, petroleum is a tool that can be used to launch Russia as a renewed great power, allowing it to acquire considerable authority in the regions that made up the former Soviet Union. While Washington favors the rapid development of Russian petroleum because it provides an alternative for the West to Middle Eastern supplies, the Bush administration has been wary of policies that can reconstitute Russia as an economic and therefore military threat. While George W. Bush and Vladimir Putin made a great show of their personal friendship in the early days of the Bush presidency, this was soon followed by much frostier relations. At the heart of the tensions was petroleum.

The battle over oil from the Caspian Sea region has involved selling arms to governments and to political movements intent on overthrowing governments. It involved major petroleum companies that were determined to cash in on the potential bonanza. And it involved battles over the pipeline routes that would be used to ship the oil to market. While the Russians wanted the petroleum from Azerbaijan to flow into their pipeline system and to markets from there, the US opposed the Russian route for this Caspian region oil. The preferred US route was to build a pipeline through

Georgia and Turkey, the latter a staunch American ally and a member of NATO. The pipeline would carry the petroleum to a Turkish Mediterranean port and from there, by tanker, to markets.

During the late 1990s, the Americans poured money into the region and feted the leaders of the Caspian Sea states at White House dinners. To make the pipeline economically viable — its price tag was $3.1 billion — the petroleum companies told Washington that government money would be needed. The US, UK, Japan and Turkey agreed to subsidize the project. In 1999, President Bill Clinton journeyed to Istanbul to initial the deal for the pipeline construction.[2]

The Baku-Tbilisi-Ceyhan (BTC) pipeline, now completed, is one of the largest post-Soviet engineering projects. In May 2005, it began the delivery of oil along its 1,776-kilometer (1,104-mile) length from the Baku fields to the Mediterranean. The pipeline, operated by BP, included the participation of British, French, American, Italian, Japanese and Norwegian companies, as well as the State Oil Company of Azerbaijan. It is expected to ship 1 million barrels of oil daily by 2008.

The pipeline is an economic, but also a political, venture. With Washington calling the shots in the background, a route that is secure from a Western point of view has been selected in preference to alternative and shorter routes through Russia or Iran.

Raising the stakes still higher in this contest over pipeline routes was the question of how the petroleum of Kazakhstan, the largest producer in the region, would

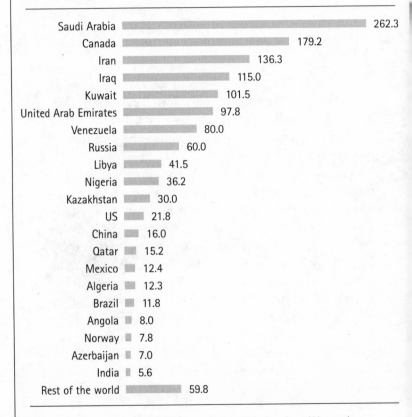

Proven Oil Reserves 2007
(billions of barrels)
Total: 1,317.5

Saudi Arabia	262.3
Canada	179.2
Iran	136.3
Iraq	115.0
Kuwait	101.5
United Arab Emirates	97.8
Venezuela	80.0
Russia	60.0
Libya	41.5
Nigeria	36.2
Kazakhstan	30.0
US	21.8
China	16.0
Qatar	15.2
Mexico	12.4
Algeria	12.3
Brazil	11.8
Angola	8.0
Norway	7.8
Azerbaijan	7.0
India	5.6
Rest of the world	59.8

Note: These figures include oil in the form of oil sands in Canada and Venezuela.
Source: PennWell Corporation, *Oil & Gas Journal*, Vol. 104.47 (December 18, 2006), US
Energy Information Administration.

flow to markets. Washington proposed that Kazakhstan (located on the eastern side of the Caspian Sea) and the major petroleum companies should jointly construct a pipeline beneath the Caspian to link up with the BTC pipeline to Turkey. Some oil from Kazakh sources is now reaching markets via Russian pipelines, but the proposal to hook Kazakhstan up with the BTC route remains a live option.

The US power play in the region was stepped up by the administration of President George W. Bush in the aftermath of the terror attacks on New York and Washington. Ostensibly to aid in its invasion of Afghanistan, Washington sent US forces to Kyrgyzstan and Uzbekistan. But when the Taliban government in Afghanistan was driven from power — much to the annoyance of Moscow — the US decided to keep forces in these countries indefinitely. The United States also provided military instructors to Georgia. These moves helped tighten the American grip on the oil-rich Caspian Sea region.

In addition to the struggles between the Americans and the Russians to control the petroleum of the former Soviet republics in the Caspian Sea region, there have been ferocious battles over Russian petroleum itself. According to the rules established by the Russian government, foreign firms are allowed to participate in the country's petroleum sector. Despite this, the regulations and the tax system strongly favor domestic firms over foreign ones. On top of that, the Russian state, under the Putin administration, has fought to put the petroleum industry back under state control and out of Russian entrepreneurs' hands.

The struggle between the Kremlin and the entrepreneurs came to a head in October 2003 with the arrest of Mikhail Khodorkovsky, the chairman and chief executive officer of Yukos, the largest privately owned petroleum company in Russia. Khodorkovsky was charged and convicted of tax evasion. Most observers believe that what led to the prosecution and imprisonment of Yukos's CEO was that he was perceived as threatening the power of Vladimir Putin. Since his imprisonment, most of the assets of Yukos have been acquired by the state-owned oil company Rosneft, at prices well below their market value.

Foreign firms have also felt the bite of Putin's power. In December 2006, in what was seen as a politically motivated power play, a consortium led by Shell Oil was pressured into selling its majority share in the $20-billion Sakhalin II natural gas project to the Russian state-owned natural gas giant, Gazprom. The Sakhalin project is developing natural gas reserves under the Pacific Ocean off Siberia's eastern coast. Russian regulators have come down heavily, as well, on British Petroleum, which has been involved in a $20-billion gas field investment near Lake Baikal and on the French company Total, which has been developing a project near the Barents Sea. These cases are seen by observers as motivated by the desire of the Russian state to increase its control in the petroleum sector.

Moscow has also flexed its muscles vis-à-vis former

Soviet republics that depend on imports of Russian petroleum. In January 2007, the Russians shut down their petroleum pipeline to Belarus for three days to drive home their demand for a higher price for their natural gas. In 2006, the Kremlin briefly halted natural gas shipments to Ukraine in a bid for higher prices. Since the pipeline that delivers gas to Ukraine continues west to provide fuel to other European countries, the dispute alarmed the European Union. In Germany, the biggest importer of Russian natural gas, the disruption of natural gas delivery to Ukraine caused the pressure in their gas pipeline to fall alarmingly. At the height of winter, German consumers were threatened with having their fuel supply cut off. As a consequence, prices of natural gas on daily markets soared until Moscow relented and renewed the flow of gas.

At present, the twenty-seven member states of the European Union import about half of the oil and natural gas they consume. By 2030, when most of the readily accessible North Sea petroleum will have been consumed, it is estimated that the EU will have to import 90 percent of its petroleum. (North Sea oil, whose deposits are owned by Norway, the UK and Denmark, amount to proven reserves of 16.3 billion barrels, about 1.6 percent of global proven reserves.)[3]

Not only is the EU headed toward ever greater dependency on imported petroleum at prices that are bound to rise over time, its member states approach the question of managing energy needs from profoundly different perspectives. For instance, Germany is committed to phasing out its nuclear plants as a source of electricity. This will make Germany relatively more dependent on imported petroleum over the middle-term future. France, on the other hand, plans to rely on nuclear power to meet 80 percent of its electricity requirements into the indefinite future.

Each of the major European countries has pursued its own distinct path to energy security and each continues to see the issue largely in national rather than in European terms.

The British, as we have seen, played a decisive role in creating two of the seven sisters, Shell and BP. Throughout the twentieth century, the British state worked closely with the major companies (it owned BP) to carve out secure supplies of petroleum for the British navy and for British industry and consumers. This strategy took it into Iran and other regions of the Middle East as well as Mexico.

After decades of relying on petroleum imports from across the seas, Britain, along with other northern European countries, was blessed with the discovery and development of North Sea petroleum. The rise of North Sea oil output transformed Aberdeen in northern Scotland into a thriving oil town. The onset of production from this new source was instrumental during the early 1980s in creating the glut on global markets that broke the power of the OPEC cartel and brought about a dramatic decline in world petroleum prices.

North Sea oil production peaked in 1999 at 4.5 million barrels a day. By 2006, production had dropped to

2.9 million barrels a day and is expected to decline further to 2.6 million barrels a day by 2010. Higher oil prices in recent years have generated a significant increase in exploration for new sources in the North Sea, a petroleum region where production costs are inherently higher than on land, and new finds have been made. Despite the new finds, however, the prognosis is that North Sea production has passed its peak and will continue to decline. For the next decade or two Britain will be blessed with supplies as well as revenues from its North Sea deposits, but after that this source will have been largely depleted.

Looking to a time when North Sea oil will be in decline as a source of energy, the government of the United Kingdom has established a plan to generate 10 percent of its electricity from renewable sources by 2012. The accounting firm of Ernst & Young reported in 2006, however, that Britain was not on track to meet this target. "The UK has Europe's best wind, wave and tidal resources yet it continues to miss out on its economic potential," said Jonathan Johns, head of renewable energy at Ernst & Young.

Germany, unlike the UK, depends almost entirely on imports (to the tune of nearly 95 percent) to meet its petroleum requirements. Germany is the third-greatest oil importer in the world — the top two are the US and Japan, and the next two following Germany are South Korea and France. German petroleum imports come mainly from Russia, Norway, the United Kingdom and Libya. Despite moderate economic growth, Germany managed to reduce the amount of petroleum it consumes by about 8 percent annually over the past decade. According to current forecasts, Germany will consume about 12 percent less petroleum in 2020 than it did in 2003. Although an emphasis on greater efficiency and on conservation has taken Germany further than most countries in cutting back on the need for fuel, the reliance on Russian petroleum imports provokes considerable anxiety in the country about the reliability of Russian sources. In spite of the anxiety, Germany has made a deal with Russia for the construction of a natural gas pipeline to connect the country to Russian supplies. The pipeline, to traverse the floor of the Baltic Sea, will bypass Poland, a fact that has provoked resentment among Poles, who see themselves being bypassed both economically and politically in this arrangement.

While oil consumption is declining in Germany, natural gas consumption is increasing and is expected to continue to increase over the next couple of decades. German oil reserves are tiny, but the country does have a moderate supply of natural gas on its own soil. Despite that, Germany imports 75 percent of the natural gas it consumes, mostly from Russia, the Netherlands and Norway. As the country phases out its nuclear power plants, it is expected that the need for natural gas will grow. In addition to natural gas, used to produce electric power, Germany relies heavily on "brown coal," or lignite coal, for the production of electric power. Three-quarters of the brown coal consumed in Germany — it is not a particularly clean fuel — is used to generate electric power.

While Germany depends on coal and natural gas for the production of electricity, it has also gone further than other European countries in the development of renewable energy sources. Germany has become the world's leading generator of electricity from windmills.

France, like Germany, is overwhelmingly dependent on imported petroleum to meet its requirements. The country has small oil deposits in the region of Paris and modest natural gas reserves in the southwest. These domestic supplies meet only about 5 percent of French demand, however. French oil imports come mainly from Saudi Arabia and Norway, with the UK, Iran, Iraq, Nigeria and Russia also supplying its needs. As the third-largest electricity producer in Europe, following Russia and Germany, France helps offset its dependence on imported petroleum by generating earnings from the export of electricity to Switzerland, the UK, Germany and Italy. Despite that, the rise in petroleum prices in 2006 increased France's trade deficit and slowed its rate of economic growth.

Italy, Europe's fourth-greatest economic power, has pursued its own unique path to supplying its petroleum needs. At the center of the Italian petroleum industry in the twentieth century was Enrico Mattei, who fought as a young man on the side of the partisans against Mussolini and the fascists. Following World War II, Mattei was named head of Italy's national oil company, Agip, with initial instructions to dismantle this company, which had been established by Mussolini. Instead, Mattei decided to rebuild the company into an instrument of

French Oil Giant Plays Rough

The seven sisters have not been the only major petroleum companies to carve out oil and gas fields for themselves, using political allies where necessary to get what they want. Elf Aquitaine was a major petroleum company owned by the French state, whose purpose was to stake out petroleum reserves in Africa, the Middle East and Russia, both to assure supplies for France and to earn profits for the French state. Its role was similar to that of British Petroleum, owned by the British state.

In 1999, TotalFina, an enterprise that was itself a merger between a French and a Belgian company, acquired Elf Aquitaine to establish a new giant, TotalFinaElf.

The company specializes in going into parts of the world where the rule of law is weak and playing rough where necessary to acquire crude petroleum. Prior to the merger, Elf Aquitaine was shown, in a French judicial inquiry in the mid-1990s, to have paid huge bribes to gain access to oil reserves in Nigeria. In 1995, while being questioned at the inquiry, Elf CEO Philippe Jaffre admitted to having paid $190 million to General Sani Abacha, the dictator of Nigeria, to secure advantageous drilling rights. Jaffre also admitted that his company paid illegal commissions to the president of Gabon, Omar Bongo, and the president of Togo, Gnassingbé Eyadéma, to prod these leaders into influencing the Nigerian dictator to accede to the French company's wishes.

Elf's CEO was not embarrassed about having proffered the bribes. "The Nigerian oilfields were extraordinarily profitable," he explained to the inquiry. "The payment of illegal commissions seemed obvious, because there was no other way to reach a friendly agreement." He told the inquiry that such practice has been common over the course of French history, and that it was normal for political and business personalities to amass "fortunes for themselves and for their families and friends, and at the same time serve France."

In 1999, Elf Aquitaine was again accused of sharp practices, this time in the Asian country of Myanmar, whose government is condemned internationally for its human rights abuses. At a time when other countries were refusing to do business in Myanmar to put pressure for reform on the government, Elf was involved in constructing a natural gas pipeline in the country. The company was accused by French prosecutors of paying bribes to the Myanmese army in return for the provision of kidnapped laborers who were forced to work on the project.

Elf's admitted practices and those that remain allegations expose a world in which paying bribes to dictators and engaging in shocking labor practices are a part of the game.

Italian economic regeneration. In 1953, he engineered the creation by the Italian state of the Ente Nazionale Idrocarburi (ENI), which took control of Agip.

Mattei, who was a populist hero in postwar Italy, set about using ENI as an instrument to break the power of the major oil companies in supplying the Italian market. He made deals with countries in the Middle East and North Africa, offering them fifty-fifty partnerships to develop their oil, much better deals than the oil-producing countries were then getting from the major oil companies. ENI made powerful enemies when it entered into open competition with Jersey Standard and Shell. In 1960, after negotiating a deal to import Soviet oil and while he was aiming for a deal with China, Mattei declared that the American oil monopoly was finished. Not only did Washington have reasons to dislike him, the French far right detested him for his alleged financial aid to the cause of Algerian independence. In October 1962, during a flight from Sicily to Milan, his plane crashed during a storm. The cause of Mattei's death has remained a mystery ever since. Was the plane crash simply an accident — the official version — or was this populist, public entrepreneur, who had so many enemies, actually assassinated?

The revelations in recent years that the CIA played a covert role in European politics, especially in Italy during the postwar decades, have lent weight to the idea that Mattei may have been murdered. In Italy, the controversy continues.

For decades after Mattei's death, ENI remained in the public sector. In the early 1990s, however, at a time when many European countries were privatizing public sector companies, steps were taken to sell off a portion of ENI to private investors.

As was the case during the postwar decades, Italy now imports 95 percent of the oil it consumes, with North African, Middle Eastern and North Sea sources as the most important. Libya has been the largest source of petroleum for the Italian market.

Italy, like Germany, has decided against a reliance on nuclear power to generate electricity. About 20 percent of Italian electricity is produced from hydro sources, leaving 80 percent to be generated from thermal plants, mainly fired by oil.

Unlike the United States, Russia and China, all powers with a strong central government and pronounced military power, the European Union is a loose federation of twenty-seven states, each with its own military, foreign policy and energy strategy. In the struggle for strategic control over petroleum-producing regions and pipeline routes that favor its interests, the EU is at a distinct disadvantage. Countries like Germany must rely on their economic weight to establish a long-term reliance on a country like Russia to provide energy on reliable terms. Vulnerability reinforces the pronounced desire among many Europeans to speed the transition to a post-petroleum world.

As in the postwar decades when it was a pioneer in the use of labor-saving technologies (the use of robots among others), Sweden today is a pioneer in seeking a post-petroleum economy. In 2006 Sweden decided to completely phase out the use of petroleum as a fuel source over the next fifteen years. The Swedish government came to this radical conclusion after studying the twin problems of global warming and the onset of dwindling petroleum supplies. The Swedes believe that as the availability of petroleum declines prices will soar and that this could set off a major global economic crisis.

"Our dependency on oil should be broken by 2020," explained Mona Sahlin, Sweden's minister of sustainable development in 2006. Ms Sahlin has argued that dependency on oil is a severe problem for the world. "A Sweden free of fossil fuels would give us enormous advantages, not least by reducing the impact from fluctuations in oil prices," she said. "The price of oil has tripled since 1996."

A Swedish government official explained: "We want to be both mentally and technically prepared for a world without oil. The plan is a response to global climate change, rising petroleum prices and warnings by some experts that the world may soon be running out of oil."

A committee of scientists, public servants, industrialists, auto manufacturers, farmers and trade unionists has been set up to plan the transition of this nation of 9 million people so that it can become the world's first post-petroleum society. What makes the Swedish experiment so far-reaching is that the Swedes have already decided that they are going to phase out the use of nuclear plants to meet their electricity requirements. Making their country both post-petroleum and post-nuclear will put them in a class by themselves.

As a major manufacturer of automobiles, the Swedish government has been working with Volvo and Saab, Sweden's two auto companies, to plan the transition to the use of ethanol and other biofuels to replace gasoline. Sweden has developed plans to get the country's public sector to end any reliance on oil. Hospitals and libraries, for instance, are receiving grants to convert to alternative fuels. There are government incentives to homeowners to make the same switch for their houses. The forest products industry has already embarked on the use of bark to generate power, and sawmills are burning sawdust to meet their energy needs.

Overall, Sweden is well down the road to a new energy system. While in 1970, 77 percent of the country's energy requirements were met by oil, by 2003 this reliance had been reduced to 32 percent. By that date, 26 percent of Swedish energy needs were being met by renewable fuels compared with a 6 percent average for the whole of the European Union.

Another European country, Iceland, is also making plans to shift away from the use of oil, although not as speedily as Sweden. By 2050, Iceland hopes to power all of its land and sea vehicles with renewable hydrogen produced by electricity generated from renewable sources.

With the largest single economy in the world, the EU is being pressured by the other world giants to develop an energy strategy that is European in scope. As their own petroleum resources are being depleted and they increasingly rely on troubled regions such as the Middle East and the Caspian Sea, Europeans are embarking on a strategy to dramatically reduce their petroleum requirements. For decades, Europe has been the center of green thinking and politics in the world. Agreements such as the Kyoto accord have largely grown out of European political determination. With Sweden in the lead, Europeans are breaking new ground on the issues of climate change and energy use. Perhaps the absence of military power may be an advantage for Europe in making a transition that the whole world is being forced to consider.

Chapter 5
Oil in the Western Hemisphere

As American oil reserves began to be depleted, the reserves of petroleum in the Middle East loomed ever more important in global terms. The rising significance of Middle East oil did not mean that other sources of oil were without economic and strategic significance. As the United States government grew ever more concerned with ensuring secure petroleum supplies for the American economy and military, sources of oil in Western Hemisphere countries took on increased significance. Oil that could be imported from the region that was seen as America's backyard, in particular oil that could be imported across a land frontier, became particularly desirable.

The three most important oil-producing countries in the Western Hemisphere, apart from the United States, are Canada, Mexico and Venezuela.

Canada is now the largest single source of oil imported into the United States. In a corner of southwestern Ontario, near the town of Petrolia, the Canadian petroleum industry had its origins in the 1850s, at about the time the first oil development was taking place in Pennsylvania. In those early days, oil from Petrolia flowed to Canadian, US and even European markets. What transformed the Canadian oil industry to make it an important element in the country's economic development and a large source of oil and natural gas for US markets were the twentieth-century discoveries of petroleum in Alberta.

Early in the century, oil discoveries were made in Alberta's Turner Valley, but the modern history of the Canadian oil industry dates from the discovery of oil in 1947 at Leduc, south of Edmonton, by Imperial Oil (a subsidiary of Jersey Standard). The post-Leduc oil boom in Alberta, shared to a lesser extent in Saskatchewan and British Columbia as a result of discoveries in those provinces, led to the investment of billions of dollars by the seven sisters in the Canadian oil patch. By 1960, nonresidents owned 77.3 percent of the investments in the Canadian oil industry. Nonresident control of the industry was even higher, at 89.8 percent. Part of the reason for the very high levels of ownership and control by nonresidents was that Canadian financial institutions, with their large capital bases and their headquarters in eastern Canada, were conservative in their investments. While they hesitated about making large investments in the Alberta oil industry, the foreign-owned major petroleum companies had no such hesitations and soon acquired overwhelming dominance in the industry.

By the early 1970s, foreign investment in the Canadian petroleum industry totaled $9.8 billion and more than 91 percent of the assets and more than 95 percent of the industry's sales were accounted for by foreign-owned firms. Eighty percent of the foreign ownership of Canada's petroleum industry lay in the hands of US-based firms. Preeminent among the foreign-owned firms was Imperial Oil, the subsidiary of Exxon (Jersey Standard). Exxon owned 69.7 percent of Imperial's capital stock. Imperial was a vertically integrated petroleum company that directly, or through its own subsidiaries (of which there were forty-nine in the early 1970s), explored for and produced crude oil and natural gas, transported its products by oceangoing and lake tankers, by rail and by pipeline, refined petroleum in nine Canadian refineries and marketed its products in all regions of the country. Imperial also produced chemicals, fertilizers and a wide range of building materials. Next in importance to Imperial were Shell and Gulf, whose combined operations were a little less than those of the industry leader. Following the second and third companies in Canada was Texaco.

Foreign control of the industry shaped the way Canadian petroleum was marketed. Canadian oil was delivered from its western (usually Alberta) sources to Ontario consumers through the Interprovincial Pipeline that ran east to Manitoba and from there south to the American midwest. The line ran through the midwest south of the Great Lakes, delivering oil to US markets en route, before it reentered Canada at Sarnia, Ontario.

In 1961, the Canadian government set up a National Oil Policy that mirrored the US program for restricting imports of oil into the United States. Instead of using quotas on imports, Canada achieved the same goal by dividing up the country's market on a regional basis. East of the Ottawa Valley in eastern Ontario, the Canadian oil market would be supplied with imported oil from Venezuela and the Middle East. West of the Ottawa Valley, the market would be supplied with oil from western Canada. Between 1961, when the program went into effect and 1973, when the global oil price revolution erupted, the price of imported oil was cheaper than Canadian oil. Under these circumstances, the bulk of the large Ontario market ended up paying a price for its oil that was higher than the world price. The purpose of the program was to encourage the development of the domestic petroleum industry.

During the 1960s, Canadian oil exports to the United States quadrupled, during a period when US imports of oil from other sources doubled. While in 1959, Canadian oil accounted for only 8.3 percent of American oil imports, by 1970, they constituted more than 20 percent. The strategy of the major petroleum companies in Canada was to press the Canadian government to allow for ever larger exports of oil and natural gas to the United States. In 1972, Imperial, which led the majors in lobbying Ottawa for additional exports, included this statement in the company's annual report: "In the current debate, the export of Canada's energy resources is being questioned; in effect, we are being urged to 'bank' our petroleum resources. Our present energy reserves, using present technology, are sufficient for our requirements for several hundred years."[1]

It is important to note the astonishing bravado from the leading company about the size of Canadian petroleum reserves, because this was to be very important in the aftermath of the oil price revolution. The rise of global oil prices from $3 a barrel to $11 a barrel between December 1973 and the spring of 1974 had a dramatic effect on the policy of the major oil companies in Canada and on the energy policies of the Canadian government. Anticipating the coming rise in world oil prices, the federal government froze the price of Canadian crude oil at $3.80 a barrel in September 1973. In the spring of 1974, with the world price at $11 a barrel, Ottawa raised the price of domestic crude to $6.50 a barrel, much higher than before, but much lower than the world price.

Several months later, the National Energy Board (NEB), Canada's regulatory body on energy, held hearings on the question of how high Canadian petroleum exports ought to be. The responses from Imperial Oil and the other majors were astounding, given their optimism only a year earlier. Imperial's estimates (the company submitted a range of three) and those of the other companies were markedly more negative about the size of Canada's petroleum reserves than they had been before the price freeze. In October 1974, based on the new estimates of the petroleum companies, the NEB issued a report that warned of looming energy shortages for Canada. The report concluded that as early as 1982, Canada would be unable to meet its domestic oil needs west of the Ottawa Valley with Canadian crude. In the spring of 1976, the government of Canada produced yet another report that digested the shocking changes in estimates of Canada's petroleum reserves. The conclusion was that Canada's estimated petroleum reserves were 60 percent lower than had been thought only three years earlier.

It is easy to see what motivated the oil companies to lower their estimates so drastically. As soon as the government froze the price of oil below the world price, the companies fiercely lobbied Ottawa to let the price rise to the world level. To make their argument compelling, they began warning that without higher prices there would be little incentive for the companies to explore and develop new reserves.

The predictions of looming shortages of petroleum in Canada from the major oil companies provoked public consternation and a dramatic shift in the federal government's energy policy. Against the backdrop of increasing uncertainty about the future of Canadian petroleum, the Liberal government of Pierre Trudeau set up a working group of top bureaucrats who met with the minister of energy to consider the creation of a publicly owned national oil company. Even before the change in the estimates of the oil companies, this idea was on the table. In December 1973, as the oil price revolution was gathering force, Prime Minister Trudeau announced that Canada would establish a publicly owned oil company. As the new estimates came in from the majors, the government became evermore determined to set up the new company, Petro-Canada, as rapidly as possible. Following the federal election in the summer of 1974, in which the Liberals won back their majority in Parliament after two years of leading a minority government, the government announced that Petro-Canada would have an initial capitalization of $500 million instead of the $80 million initially considered.

In March 1975, when Energy Minister Donald Macdonald made the case in the House of Commons to create Petro-Canada, he pointed to the dramatic changes that had occurred. "It is the extent and nature of these changes," he stated, "which have in our view tipped the balance decisively in favour of federal entrepreneurship in the oil and gas industries."

A crucial reason for the creation of Petro-Canada was that the federal government no longer trusted the major foreign-owned oil companies. The advice they had received from the companies had been so obviously self-servicing that the members of the Trudeau government concluded Canada needed what was called "a window on the industry" that could be relied upon. That window would be provided by Petro-Canada. Only a major petroleum company, owned by the government of Canada, could be counted on to provide the most reliable information about the country's petroleum reserves and the future prospects of the Canadian oil industry, the government believed.

From the time it was established the plan was that Petro-Canada would be a vertically integrated company that would operate in all aspects of the petroleum business, from exploration for new oil and natural gas sources to final marketing. Because of the concerns about establishing reserves of oil and natural gas to meet Canadian needs, Petro-Canada was to become actively involved in exploration for petroleum in nontraditional areas, such as the Northwest Territories, offshore regions in the Arctic and off the coast of Newfoundland, and in the development of nonconventional sources, principally the oil sands in northern Alberta. Under the legislation setting it up, Petro-Canada was empowered to undertake acquisitions of existing petroleum companies, which it soon did.

In 1976, Petro-Canada purchased the Canadian assets of Atlantic Richfield for $342 million. Two years later, the company took over the Canadian assets of the Phillips Petroleum Company for $1.5 billion, at the time the biggest corporate takeover in Canadian history. This gave Petro-Canada a total value of $2.4 billion and made it a substantial producer of oil and natural gas.

The existence of a publicly owned petroleum company was politically controversial from the outset. Even though public opinion polls showed that the majority of the population was enthusiastic about the creation of Petro-Canada and preferred public to foreign ownership of the petroleum industry, the crown corporation had powerful opponents. The presence of Petro-Canada's headquarters in Calgary, dubbed "red square," was detested by the city's private-sector oilmen. The Progressive Conservative party, led by Joe Clark, was committed to privatizing many crown corporations when it took office as a minority government in May 1979. During the short duration of the Clark government — it was defeated by the Liberals, under Pierre Trudeau, in February 1980 — a Conservative task force recommended that Petro-Canada be broken in two, with the profitable parts privatized (each individual Canadian citizen would receive shares in the company). Meanwhile, the debts of the company and its long-term, high-risk exploration ventures would remain in the public sector. With the return of the Liberals to power, talk of privatizing Petro-Canada ceased, but only for the time being.

In 1980, the Trudeau government unveiled the National Energy Program (NEP), whose purpose was to achieve 50 percent Canadian ownership of the petroleum industry by 1990. The policy set out to reach this goal both through the expansion of Petro-Canada and through the encouragement of the development of large, privately owned Canadian oil companies.

In line with the policy of expanding Petro-Canada, in 1981, the crown company purchased the assets of Petrofina Canada, the subsidiary of its Belgian parent company, for $1.5 billion, acquiring among other things, the company's chain of over one thousand service stations in eastern Canada. The following year, Petro-Canada bought out the refining and marketing operations of British Petroleum for $400 million. A Gallup poll taken in October 1982 revealed that 72 percent of Canadians were in favor of Petro-Canada's involvement in exploration; 44 percent in its involvement in international purchases; and 63 percent in its involvement in retail sales.[2]

To increase private Canadian ownership in the petroleum industry, the NEP overhauled the petroleum sector's tax system. Under the new system, depletion allowances for development expenditures in oil and gas fields were eliminated and depletion allowances for exploration were phased out. (Depletion allowances enabled oil companies to write off much of their income provided they continued to invest in development and exploration.) Eliminating these tax incentives effectively raised the level of tax payable by the oil companies. Replacing depletion allowances was a new incentive program that was directly linked to the achievement of a higher level of private sector Canadian ownership, the Petroleum Incentives Program (PIP). The PIP grant system was designed to funnel the additional cash flowing to the government from the increased tax on the industry into the coffers of companies investing in development and exploration, according to the degree of their Canadian ownership.

A week after the announcement of the NEP, Ronald Reagan was elected president of the United States. Even before Reagan's election, the Carter administration had lashed out at the NEP. After Reagan was sworn in as president on January 20, 1981, his administration undertook a concerted attack on the NEP, charging that it discriminated against American-owned petroleum companies.

While the NEP did result in the investment of billions of dollars in Petro-Canada and privately owned Canadian petroleum companies, it fell prey both to the dramatic plunge in petroleum prices that began in 1982 and to the continuing political offensive against it. In September 1984, for reasons that had little to do with the NEP, Brian Mulroney led the Progressive Conservative party to office in a sweeping electoral victory.

The Mulroney government acted decisively to eliminate the NEP and to negotiate the Canada-US Free Trade Agreement, which transformed the role of Canada as a supplier of petroleum to the United States. The Mulroney government dismantled the NEP, eliminating the PIP grants, thereby ending this attempt to increase Canadian private ownership in the petroleum industry. The Conservatives also halted the further growth of Petro-Canada through the acquisition of the Canadian assets of foreign-owned oil companies. In addition, as the world price of oil fell, the Mulroney government scrapped the system of controls on the domestic price of petroleum.

In the lead-up to the 1988 federal election, the Mulroney government negotiated a comprehensive free trade agreement with the United States. Following the Conservative victory in the election, the Canada-US Free Trade Agreement (FTA) took effect on January 1, 1989. It included a number of measures that completely changed the terms on which Canada exported petroleum to the United States. The FTA was drafted by negotiators in both Canada and the United States who were hostile to the NEP and who were determined to ensure that no program of its kind was ever launched again by the Canadian federal government.

Under the terms of the FTA, Canada undertook not to put into place a two-price system for its petroleum. That meant if Canada sold oil to the United States at the world price, there could not be a lower domestic price in Canada. In addition, one of the provisions of the FTA, which applied to all sectors and not just petroleum, was that henceforth Canada had to extend what was called "national treatment" to American-owned firms. This meant that in future Canada could not establish tax or subsidy programs that discriminated in favor of domestically owned firms and against American-owned firms. The consequence of this feature of the FTA was that there could be no repeat of the NEP's PIP grant system. Finally, and most dramatically, the FTA established that in the event of a global petroleum shortage, Canada would be obligated to continue exporting oil to the United States. Canada undertook to go on exporting as much oil as it had been exporting over the preceding three years even if a world crisis reduced or eliminated oil imports into North America from elsewhere. Should such a situation materialize, Canada would have to ship oil to the US before seeing to the needs of the parts of eastern Canada that would go short because of reduced imports.

The FTA gave the United States highly privileged access to Alberta oil. In some ways, that entrée was even more privileged than was the access enjoyed by eastern Canada.

In the nearly two decades since the FTA and later the North American Free Trade Agreement (NAFTA) went into effect, the American reliance on Canadian oil has grown steadily larger. As oil, national security and the war on terror have become evermore tightly aligned in the thinking of American political leaders, Canada's largest petroleum deposit, the oil sands, has been more closely scrutinized from Washington. Located across an enormous region of northeastern Alberta — in three major areas spread over 140,800 square kilometers (54,367 square miles), an area larger than the state of Florida — centered on Fort McMurray, about 300 kilometers (186 miles) north of Edmonton, the oil sands contain almost as much oil as the conventional reserves of Saudi Arabia.

In the late 1990s and the early years of the twenty-first century, petroleum companies invested $24.7 billion in the development of oil sands production. Alberta's petroleum production has become increasingly centered on the oil sands as conventional reserves are depleted. In 2003, more than 52 percent of the province's total crude oil and equivalent production came from the oil sands. By that year, oil sands production reached 858,000 barrels a day. Since then the output of oil from this source has risen to account for half of Canada's crude output and 10 percent of North America's crude production.

The problem is that this oil is very expensive to extract and that producing oil from the oil sands involves strip mining on a vast scale and the reduction of huge tracts of land to a scarred horror. In addition, the production of oil from the oil sands requires enormous inputs of fresh water and natural gas. Moreover, the industrial process by which the oil is separated from the sand results in the release of large quantities of greenhouse gases into the atmosphere.[3]

In July 2006, at 1.6 million barrels a day, Canada was the largest single exporter of crude oil to the United

States. Rounding out the top five exporters to the US were Mexico with just over 1.5 million barrels daily, Saudi Arabia at over 1.2 million barrels, Venezuela with nearly 1.2 million barrels, and Nigeria with just over 1 million barrels. These five countries were the sources of 66 percent of American oil imports. What these totals make clear is the high dependence of the United States on Canada and other Western Hemisphere sources of oil and its relatively low reliance on Middle Eastern sources in comparison with Western Europe and Japan, which depend much more on the Middle East.

Mexico, the second-largest source of oil imports for the US, has long been an important petroleum-producing country. Much of Mexico's oil reserves were developed by an Englishman, Weetman Pearson, a contractor from Yorkshire, who arrived on the scene at the invitation of Mexico's dictator, Porfirio Díaz, at the end of the nineteenth century. The Díaz government had engaged Pearson to build a canal to drain Mexico City. Following further harbor and transportation ventures, he was inspired by the Texas Spindletop discovery in 1901 to buy oil concessions on promising terrain in Mexico. After spending £5 million on exploration, Pearson struck it big, with major petroleum discoveries in 1908. He went on to form the Mexican Eagle (Aguila) petroleum company and after fighting it out with a Standard Oil subsidiary, Pearson ended up dominating the Mexican oil industry. In recognition of the company he built, which became a crucial supplier of oil to the Royal Navy, Pearson received a peerage and became Lord Cowdray.

The paramount position occupied by Cowdray's company provoked the ire of the United States and bitter diplomatic exchanges ensued between the Americans and the British about the politics of Mexican oil. In 1919, Lord Cowdray sold the bulk of his petroleum holdings to Shell Oil. During the 1920s and 1930s, the British and the Americans continued their battles over control of Mexican oil. In the 1920s, Mexico became the leading oil-exporting country in the world.

In the mid-1930s, Mexican oil workers, who experienced appalling conditions in the hovels and shantytowns in which they lived and worked, went on strike. Demands were made that the foreign-owned oil companies should take steps to improve conditions, something the companies stubbornly refused to do. On March 18, 1938, the government of Lázaro Cárdenas, responding to the nationalist revulsion against the oil companies, nationalized the seventeen foreign-owned petroleum companies operating in the country. The day was celebrated as a second Mexican declaration of independence.

The oil companies sought retaliatory intervention from the Roosevelt administration. But FDR stayed his hand, affirming that the "United States would show no sympathy to rich individuals who [had] obtained large land holdings in Mexico for virtually nothing."[4]

To take the place of the foreign-owned companies, the government of Mexico established a publicly owned enterprise, Pemex, a company that assumed an important symbolic status as an expression of the Mexican nation. In retaliation against Mexico's nationalization of its assets, the major oil companies took concerted action to shut Mexican oil out of world markets. They hoped that the blow to Mexican exports of oil would bring the Mexican government back into line. They assumed, as well, that without their technical expertise Pemex would founder and fail. While they succeeded in shutting Mexican oil out of world markets, they were wrong about Pemex. Initially the company suffered as a result of corruption and because it lacked sufficient engineers and technicians. But Pemex overcame these problems and succeeded in producing oil for the Mexican market.

Eventually Mexico was forced to pay $130 million in compensation for the takeover of the companies. The Anglo-American boycott of Mexican oil was called off during World War II.

The oil giants moved on from Mexico to Venezuela, whose dictatorial government welcomed them. In the early postwar period, Venezuela had become the world's second-largest oil-producing nation, next to the United States.

During the 1920s and 1930s, Venezuela was transformed by the development of its oil riches. Jersey Standard, Shell and Gulf were the three majors that played the largest role in the Venezuelan oil patch. Petroleum exports made Venezuela the richest country in South America. Its capital city, Caracas, experienced explosive growth during the interwar years, and its streets were crowded with automobiles. As with other countries that had been touched by the gift of oil, however, the share of the spoils was extremely unequal. The oil companies reaped huge profits and Venezuela's dictator Juan Vicente Gómez (in power from 1908 until his death in 1935) and those close to his regime, including the army, shared in the spoils. But oil wealth did nothing to alleviate the poverty of the majority of Venezuelans. Indeed, by raising prices, the oil boom actually deepened the distress experienced by most of the population.

The death of Gomez was followed by popular discontent, widespread looting and the killing of members of the dictator's family. Following the demise of the Gomez regime, Venezuelan politics entered a turbulent period in which a movement toward the establishment of democracy was interrupted periodically with violent interludes and the intrusion of the military into the running of the country.

In 1938, the Venezuelan government, responding to popular demand for a sharing of the spoils of the profits from petroleum that were flowing to the foreign-owned oil companies, demanded that the companies' contracts be revised. The government wanted higher royalties and taxes and in return for this, it offered the companies a forty-year renewal of their right to operate in Venezuela. Shell was prepared to go along with the reforms, while Jersey Standard, at first, resisted them. In the end, with the mediation of Herbert Hoover (son of the former US president of the same name), a compromise was reached. The companies obtained their forty-year contracts and paid higher royalties.[5]

The march toward democracy brought a reformist party, the Acción Democrática (AD), to power. The new government's oil minister, Pérez Alfonso, who played a key role in the establishment of OPEC in the late 1950s, believed that Venezuela needed a new deal with the companies in return for the depletion of its nonrenewable petroleum reserves. His rallying cry, soon to resonate in other countries in the Western Hemisphere, and in the Persian Gulf, was that the government should have a fifty-fifty share in all the profits from the industry. In November 1948, the government passed a law embodying the fifty-fifty concept, and although Alfonso was briefly removed from office by a coup, the law went into effect. The Venezuelan government had succeeded in achieving 50 percent ownership of the country's petroleum industry, with the other half remaining in the hands of the major petroleum companies.[6]

In the 1950s, the progress toward democracy was again halted when a military junta seized power. The junta pursued policies that were to the liking of the foreign-owned oil companies. In Washington, the Eisenhower administration looked with favor on the junta and its pro-American stance. In 1958, the junta's power was broken and new elections were called. The winner of the presidential election, the AD's Rómulo Betancourt, was inaugurated in February 1959.

With Betancourt's democratic regime in power, the Venezuelan government took the lead in organizing the world's oil-exporting countries to work together to win a better deal for the oil from the major petroleum companies. In 1960, the major oil exporters founded OPEC. The cartel's goal was to halt falling oil prices and to ensure higher returns to its members from the sale of their oil to the world's great industrial powers who were the largest importers.

During the 1970s, at a time when Middle Eastern countries insisted on state ownership of large parts of their petroleum industries, Venezuela nationalized its own oil industry, placing the holdings of the foreign companies under the administrative supervision of a state-owned entity, Petróleos de Venezuela, SA (PDVSA). In return for the surrender of their assets, the fourteen foreign-owned firms received $1 billion in compensation. To operate the country's petroleum industry following nationalization, what had been the operations of the fourteen firms were reorganized into four functioning units, structured around the holdings of the four largest foreign-owned firms. The PDVSA oversaw the running of these units. While nationalization helped foster the rise of a rather narrow elite in Venezuela that benefited from it, the mass of the population still saw few improvements in their own lives. Indeed, while the creation of the PDVSA placed greater authority over the running of the industry in the hands of the Venezuelan state, it did not eliminate the continuing role and profitability of the majors in the country.

At the end of the twentieth century, at a time when political movements in Latin America were stirring in opposition to the free enterprise model in their countries that promoted wealthy elites and poverty-stricken majorities, a remarkable new regime came to power in Venezuela. In 1998, Hugo Chávez, a former army officer, whose platform, including a pledge to reorganize the PDVSA and redistribute the oil wealth to the majority, won an overwhelming victory in his bid for the presidency of Venezuela.

Chávez's political support was particularly strong in the poor townships that surrounded Caracas. The new president was determined to use profits from oil sales to fund large-scale new health care and educational programs. Opposing him were the wealthy and the middle classes in the capital, who could count on the privately owned media to take their side. The opponents of Chávez wanted to privatize the PDVSA as a way to bolster their privileged positions in the social order.

The fate of the country's oil industry was at the center of the political struggles that ensued in the highly polarized country. In 1999, President Chávez submitted a new constitution to the voters. The proposed constitution, massively ratified in a referendum, included a provision that forbade the privatization of the PDVSA.

The direction taken by the Chávez regime provoked a highly negative response from Washington, particularly after the installation of George W. Bush as president in January 2001. In December 2001, the Venezuelan opposition, with the evident backing of Washington, launched a general strike whose goal was to force Chávez from power. One motive for the move to topple a democratically elected government was the promulgation of a law, to take effect on January 1, 2003, that would double the royalties paid to the government by foreign-owned oil companies, the largest among them ExxonMobil. The opposition committed itself to privatizing the PDVSA and rescinding the move to double royalties for foreign-owned oil companies.

The general strike was followed by a direct attempt to oust Chávez from power. In April 2002, a coup hatched by Venezuelan business leaders and military officers forced the president out of power for two days, before he was reinstalled by a popular movement that compelled those who had seized power to stand down. The precise role of Washington in the failed coup is not yet known. What is clear is that US intelligence was well informed about the nature of the impending coup. Given the long history of American involvement in overturning regimes in Central and South America, no one would be shocked a few years from now to learn that the Bush administration was actively involved in planning the operation in Venezuela. The difference, of course, was that this attempt to eliminate Chávez failed, as did a subsequent effort to remove him in a referendum.

Evidence of one kind of American intervention in the Venezuelan political process did emerge following the failed coup attempt. It was revealed that the National Endowment for Democracy (NED), an agency of the US government, poured nearly $900,000 into the coffers of the opposition in Venezuela in the year prior to the coup.

In 2005, Chávez forged a major energy deal with China. Everywhere the Americans look these days they encounter the Chinese who are avidly competing for available oil on the international market. The days are gone when the United States can assume that Western

Hemisphere oil is a special American preserve that can be drawn on at will. Chávez has gained appreciable power by being able to sell oil to China and to others and to earn the means to fund popular programs that benefit his power base among Venezuela's lower classes, as well as to purchase armaments. Chávez has not only thrown American military advisers out of Venezuela, he has warned Washington that American efforts to destabilize his regime will be met with an oil embargo against the US. In March 2005, when Chávez purchased weapons from Russia, US Defense Secretary Donald Rumsfeld questioned his motives: "I can't imagine why Venezuela needs 100,000 AK-47's."[7]

The Chávez government used its petroleum revenues not only to meet economic and social objectives at home but to pursue political goals abroad. Chávez has sold off billions of dollars worth of US securities and provided low-interest loans to Argentina, Ecuador and other Latin American countries. Venezuela also sold oil to Cuba and Haiti at a discount. Through its ownership of the petroleum company CITGO, which operates gas stations in the United States, Venezuela offered aid to the poor in the Bronx, as well as to the victims of Hurricane Katrina in New Orleans. To help Latin American countries reduce their dependence on capital from the International Monetary Fund (IMF) and the World Bank — customarily loaned with socioeconomic strings attached — Venezuela has set up the International Humanitarian Bank. The bank arranged to ship Venezuelan oil to a refinery in Uruguay in return for payment in cattle. In a similar undertaking, Venezuelan oil was swapped for cattle and medical equipment from Argentina. Under Chávez, Venezuelan oil is being used to undermine the sway of the US and its oil companies in a region that has perennially experienced American domination. The revised National Security Strategy of the United States, released in March 2002, charged that: "In Venezuela, a demagogue awash in oil money is undermining democracy and seeking to destabilize the region."

Chapter 6
Peak Oil and Global Warming

Two great issues loom over the future of the global petroleum industry. First there is the question of "peak oil;" second there is the rising concern about greenhouse gas emissions and global warming.

There are widely differing estimates about the extent of the world's petroleum reserves, and about how much oil can be produced using enhanced recovery techniques (to extract more oil from producing fields) and how much can be produced from nonconventional sources, such as oil sands, oil shales and the liquefaction of coal. All agree, however, on the basic fact that petroleum reserves are finite and that the world cannot rely indefinitely on the massive consumption of oil and natural gas to meet its energy needs.

In the last few years, the term "peak oil" has been used to characterize the seriousness of this issue. Peak oil refers to the point at which the world's petroleum output reaches its maximum level. The broad concept of peak oil can be grasped through the employment of a bell curve, a curve that slopes upward to its zenith and then slopes

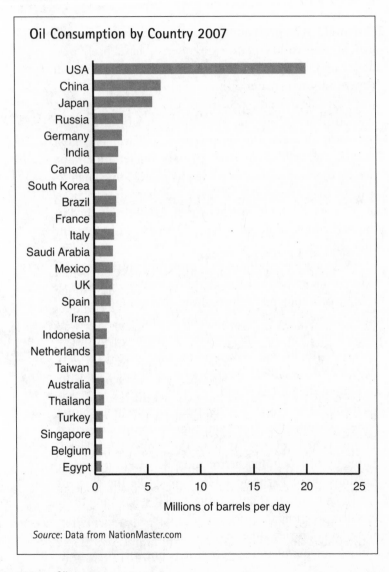

Oil Consumption by Country 2007

Country	Millions of barrels per day

Source: Data from NationMaster.com

downward. The peak point of the curve is reached when half of the world's petroleum reserves have been produced and consumed. From this point, production will flatten out for a greater or lesser period of time, and then will begin its descent. Because of the very high demand for petroleum in our era, in comparison with the industry's early decades, the downward curve will be much sharper and will occur over a much briefer timeframe than it took for output to rise to its peak. Some analysts believe that the point of peak oil has already been reached, while others anticipate that it will be attained in the next couple of decades. Some estimates put the point later still.

The concept of peak oil has provoked an intense dialogue in many parts of the world on the implications of a future without oil. Approaching that ominous point, two vital avenues of inquiry have opened up. The first focuses on how to conserve the remaining petroleum reserves by reducing consumption. The second involves the search for viable alternative sources of energy for the coming of the oil-less world.

It should be noted that the peak oil question is not a purely scientific one free from inputs from sources that have a vested interest in how the issue is perceived. Estimates of remaining petroleum reserves, in particular locations, have a considerable impact on the flow of investments into particular projects. They have an effect, as well, on petroleum prices. Since oil producers, companies and countries alike, have a tangible interest in the outlook for petroleum supplies, it is not surprising that they use self-serving estimates in the struggle for their own economic well-being. Making this even less transparent is the ability of major producing countries to decrease or increase their production of petroleum with the express purpose of affecting the price. One basic purpose of a producers' cartel such as OPEC has been to get producing countries to agree to quotas to limit their production. Limiting production in order to drive up the price of oil, and therefore, the return to producers, has been OPEC's basic function. It has, on occasion, been alleged that major producing countries, such as Saudi Arabia, have increased petroleum production to push down petroleum prices, not only to prevent the importing countries from sinking into a recession but to influence the outcome of US elections. It is well known that a US administration benefits politically from a drop in gasoline prices in the several months leading up to presidential or congressional elections.

The essential point, however, is that while market manipulations of this sort can obscure long-term trends, they do not affect the underlying fact that oil supplies are finite and that they are running out.

Conservation, the reduction of the amount of energy consumed, and bringing on stream new sources of energy are the key ways societies must adapt to the prospect of peak oil. Three sets of impulses promote conservation. The first is the price mechanism. Within a market system, as goods become scarce while demand remains elevated, prices are driven up. The consequence is that consumers try to reduce their use of the high-priced commodity. For instance, higher gasoline prices motivate reduced use of automobiles, greater reliance on public transit and falling sales of gas-guzzling vehicles such as SUVs in favor of more fuel efficient, smaller vehicles. Taxi drivers and others who need to put huge mileage on their vehicles are motivated to consider hybrid (gasoline and electric-battery-powered) vehicles. For them, the calculation is that the higher price of the vehicle is more than offset by its much lower fuel bill. While the price mechanism pushes society toward conservation, it does so in a notably unequal way. Those with high disposable incomes are much less inclined to heed the market signal of high gasoline prices than those with low incomes. While the affluent may continue to drive SUVs in times of high prices, poor rural residents often have no access to public transit and are forced to keep driving and to make other painful lifestyle choices such as skimping on high quality food or turning down the thermostats in their homes during the winter.

One common effect of the use of the price mechanism to achieve conservation is that commodities that were once widely available to most people become more or less limited to the affluent. Such a system, particularly when employed worldwide, results in a highly unequal distribution of the use of the planet's resources, based on wealth.

The way in which energy resource rationing is happening can be seen by examining the per capita carbon dioxide emissions of different societies (these emissions are the direct consequence of levels of energy consumption.)

While the energy consumption of the average person in the world produces a little more than one metric ton of carbon annually (measured in carbon dioxide emissions), this average disguises enormous differences. Annual per capita carbon emissions in the United States total 20 metric tons, in Canada, 18.4 metric tons, Japan, 9.8 metric tons, France, 6.8 metric tons, and Sweden, 6.1 metric tons. By contrast, the average person in developing countries is responsible for the emission of .5 metric tons. The average American accounts for the emission of eighteen times as much carbon dioxide as the average Indian and ninety-nine times as much as the average inhabitant of Bangladesh.[1]

These figures point to other factors at work in addition to different levels of income from country to country. The first countries on the list are all wealthy countries with high per capita incomes. But energy use varies considerably between the US and Sweden, for example. At work, in addition to the price mechanism, are two other influential factors: the impact of government policies and the effect of societal attitudes.

Government regulations of various kinds have been used to promote energy conservation, among other objectives. Gasoline taxes have been an important source of revenue for road and highway construction, as well as for other government programs, since the 1920s. In addition to providing funds for government programs, such taxes increase the price of gasoline, thereby discouraging its use. The higher the tax, the more its second function, promoting conservation, kicks in. In Europe where gasoline taxes are much higher than in Canada and the United States, the promotion of conservation this way has been a major policy objective for decades. On average, even as prices have risen sharply in North America, Europeans continue to pay about twice as much for their gasoline, the difference accounted for by higher taxes.

To illustrate how this works, let's look at the costs that go into the price of gasoline purchased at the pumps. Included in the end price of a liter or a gallon of gas are the following elements:

- exploration for crude oil
- price of crude oil
- payment of royalties, taxes and profits to producing country (as well as states and provinces in the US and Canada)
- transportation by tankers, pipelines and rail to refineries
- production of gasoline at refinery
- transportation of the end product to service stations
- markup for the retailer (can be an independent or a subsidiary of a major oil company)
- gasoline tax
- corporate income tax paid by the companies involved in the production process
- profit to the oil company, which is divided into two parts, dividends to shareholders and retained earnings.

The two biggest items on the list are the price of crude

oil and the gasoline tax. In 2006, about 60 percent of the price drivers paid at the pump in France was collected in tax by the government. In California, the tax paid at the pump was 21 percent. In Canada, the tax paid by the consumer at the gas station varies from province to province (or territory). The average tax paid by Canadian drivers at the pump is about 25 percent. This includes the provincial or territorial gas tax, which ranged (in 2006) from a low of 6.2¢/liter in New Brunswick to a high of 16.5¢/liter in Newfoundland and Labrador. On top of this there is often a provincial sales tax and in large urban centers, a transit tax. The federal government collects 10¢/liter in its excise tax and then charges the Goods and Services Tax (GST) at a rate of 5 percent on the total price.

To show how prices vary from country to country, it helps to translate prices into US dollars and gallons for the sake of comparison. In October 2006, after coming down from higher levels during the summer, average prices per gallon for regular gas were as follows: United States, $2.53 (67¢/liter); Canada, $2.96 (78¢/liter); United Kingdom, $6.18 ($1.63/liter); France, $5.63 ($1.49/liter); and Germany, $5.86 ($1.55/liter).

Because the tax on gasoline is so much higher in Europe than in North America, sudden spikes in the global price of crude oil have a much more dramatic proportional impact on the price of oil in the United States and Canada than in Europe. The paradoxical consequence is that gasoline price spikes provoke greater political outrage in North America than in Europe. Not that

Canadians or Americans would want to trade places with Europeans where gasoline prices are concerned.

One consequence of higher gasoline prices in Europe is that the fleet of automobiles driven there is significantly more efficient than its North American counterpart. Almost all European cars are four-cylinder vehicles, while a much higher proportion of North American cars deploy six cylinders. While the number of SUVs has been growing in Europe in recent years, these large gas-guzzling vehicles, in addition to pickup trucks, constitute a much larger proportion of the North American fleet.

In addition to fuel efficiency there is the issue of controls on automobile emissions. On emissions, California has been the world leader, blazing the trail for the setting of standards. The state's pioneer role was linked to the onset of a problem, directly related to the ubiquity of the automobile — smog. The first episodes of smog in Los Angeles that were recognized as a new and alarming phenomenon occurred during the summer of 1943, when visibility was sharply reduced and people suffered from smarting eyes, respiratory discomfort and, in some cases, nausea. Los Angeles is especially susceptible to smog because it is located in the basin of the San Fernando Valley so that automobile emissions are frequently trapped and concentrated in the lower atmosphere. Today nearly 16 million people, about half the population of the state of California, live in Los Angeles and its environs.

In 1966, the California legislature passed legislation establishing automobile tailpipe emission standards for hydrocarbons and carbon monoxide, the first controls of this type in the United States. In 1976, the state limited the lead that could be present in gasoline, a step that has since been taken throughout the industrialized world. In 1990, California established standards for cleaner burning fuels and low and zero emission vehicles (ZEVs). The regulation required that 2 percent of new vehicle sales by 1998, 5 percent by 2001 and 10 percent of large vehicles sold beginning in 2003 must be ZEVs, powered by electricity or alternative fuels, such as hydrogen, that do not pollute at all. Several times, the state decided to roll back the deadlines it had set, when auto companies insisted that they were not ready to meet the goals. In 2001, California decided to give companies credit for low emission vehicles in addition to ZEVs. This meant that hybrid cars such as the Toyota Prius and the Honda Insight, which are powered by a combination of gasoline and electricity, were included on the list of vehicles toward which the state required the auto industry to move in its future production.

California's record in pushing the auto industry toward more stringent emission standards reveals both the strength and the weakness of governments' efforts to clean up the atmosphere, both to reduce smog and to cut back on the release of greenhouse gases. A powerful state such as California with a population of more than 30 million can force industry to design vehicles that meet the standards state legislation requires. But the fact that even California has had to extend deadlines in the face of industry foot dragging reveals how difficult is the task of achieving fundamental change.

The deadly twin of the peak oil issue is the threat of catastrophic climate change. As petroleum runs out, its expanding use has been driving the increase in the release of greenhouse gases into the atmosphere. An ever wider consensus among scientists has concluded that the emission of greenhouse gases as a consequence of human activity, largely through the burning of fossil fuels, has been increasing the proportion of carbon dioxide in the earth's atmosphere. Carbon dioxide is a greenhouse gas, which means that its presence in the atmosphere causes more of the heat from the sun to be trapped. The consequence is that the temperature of the earth's surface is increasing and is projected to increase according to the mid-range estimate by an average of 3°C (5.5°F) by the year 2100. Land surfaces are projected to experience greater temperature increases than the surface of the oceans, and northern polar regions are projected to have higher than average increases.[2]

While an average increase of 3°C (5.5°F) may not sound like much, the impact on the global environment is predicted to be calamitous. Species will be driven to extinction, deserts will expand, sources of fresh water will be imperiled and sea levels will rise, flooding coastal areas and completely submerging some low-lying island states.

The interconnection between the two threats of peak oil and climate change is such that for the human race to grapple with one, it will be required to cope with the other. Coping is the topic of the concluding chapter.

Chapter 7
Unprecedented Challenges

For well over a century the petroleum industry has propelled the rise of industrial civilization. In addition, it has driven the cause of empire, military conflicts, the making of vast fortunes, and the division of the world into the privileged and the poor. In our age, two additional factors have been added to the equation. With the vast economic expansion of China and India, the world is hurtling toward the fateful moment of peak oil. And as oil supplies are depleted, industrial civilization has unleashed the prospect of catastrophic climate change.

It has fallen to us to cope with the socioeconomic consequences of past development and to plan and prepare for the coming world of decreasing oil supply and climate change. Achieving a political consensus among the nations of the world, with all their rivalries and their different levels of development, to grapple with the multifaceted crisis the petroleum age has generated, could prove to be the greatest challenge that has ever confronted humankind. The call of the political leaders of rich societies to developing countries to join in a common program to reduce greenhouse gas emissions and to practice conservation in order to husband remaining petroleum supplies is bound to be met with the response that this amounts to an unconscionable unfairness.

After more than a century of the leading countries enriching themselves from the oil fields of the world, often in wantonly wasteful fashion, the political and economic elites of developing countries are inclined to regard calls for restraint as nothing more than an attempt to block their own advance.

What makes the oil crisis so difficult is that addressing it affects so many aspects of our civilization, and the power relations within it, that to cope with its fundamentals will require what can be called a grand socioeconomic bargain of international scope. Standing in the way of such a bargain are formidable obstacles.

There are the enormous short- and middle-term benefits for the wealthy and powerful if they do nothing or next to nothing to come to grips with the crisis. Those who profit directly from the petroleum industry, the automotive industry, the manufacturers of aircraft and the world's airlines have an immense vested interest in keeping the present system going as long as possible. The top corporate executives of the major companies in these sectors, who depend for their livelihoods on the availability of petroleum, respond to the problems geologists and climatologists are pointing to in ways that are, at best, cosmetic. When gasoline prices increase sharply, auto companies respond by promoting the sale of vehicles that are more fuel efficient. In part, this is a real response to the threat that customers who feel the pinch of high fuel prices will abandon them for the more efficient vehicles of other manufacturers. And it is also good public relations in a time when the popular concern with the environment is at an all-time high. Meanwhile, major auto companies continue to churn out millions of gas-guzzling vehicles for those who can afford the price tag and the fuel bill.

Those who run major petroleum companies respond in similar ways. They mount advertising campaigns that stress their commitment to a clean environment and to the quest for sustainable sources of energy, styling themselves as energy companies that have the long-term interest of their customers at heart. When pressed further by those who are issuing ever starker warnings about what is coming in the not-too-distant future, the intellectual defenders of the corporations most linked to petroleum fall back on two main lines of argument.

First, the corporations quarrel with the science, and they have been exposed as having contributed to the "junk science" that disputes the case for global warming.[1] On the matter of petroleum supply, while not disputing the hard fact that oil supplies are finite, they insist that the day of peak oil is a long way off. The best way to meet the world's need for petroleum in an era of rapidly expanding demand is to engage in a never-ending quest for new oil and natural gas supplies, they insist. Equipped with scientific and technological tools that would have been the envy of past generations, including geological exploration from satellites in earth orbit, the argument goes, oil companies will find new supplies. Some of the new supplies, it is true, will be discovered under the sea and in polar regions where petroleum development poses the risk of severe environmental damage. While everything that can be done to avoid environmental damage must be done, the defenders argue, development must be allowed to proceed.

Proceeding from this logic, American policymakers have decided that oil development in the Gulf of Mexico and in Alaska can go ahead. In the case of the Gulf, the activities of the petroleum industry have been linked to the catastrophic degradation of the ecology of Louisiana's southern coast. Across this delicate region, sustained over the ages by a balance between the sea and the silt washed into the delta by the Mississippi River, a highly destructive process has been set in motion by invasive petroleum development. As a consequence, every ten months an area the size of Manhattan Island is being washed into the sea. At risk is the unique terrain of the bayous, swamps and thousands of life forms across a region the size of the state of Connecticut. While there is general awareness of the plight of New Orleans in the aftermath of Hurricane Katrina in 2005, the wider catastrophe in the coastal region of south Louisiana is not widely appreciated outside the area itself. In the case of Alaska, the petroleum lobby, with its powerful links to the administration of President George W. Bush, succeeded in winning approval for oil development in the delicate environment of the Arctic National Wildlife Refuge. The development was promoted as necessary because it would reduce

American dependence on imported oil. Critics pointed out that the entire project would produce a volume of oil over the next two decades that would only reduce America's import needs by about 3 percent.[2]

The orientation of policymakers in these instances is powerfully reinforced by the outlook of corporate managers whose time horizon is also a short one. Two factors are principally responsible for this perspective. The first is what can be termed the "accountant outlook." Giant corporations, especially those based in the United States, are prone to measuring success on a quarter to quarter basis. What matters to top managers and to institutional and individual investors is their performance as measured in the numbers every three months. This fixation militates against long-term planning of the kind that occurs when engineers, geologists and other scientists have greater sway. (This point has been made in analyses of why Japanese auto companies like Toyota, with their stronger emphasis on engineering and a more distant planning horizon, so regularly outperform American companies like General Motors and Ford.)

Closely tied to the accountant outlook is the career path of top executive officers of major petroleum and auto companies. Chief executive officers and other high executives are mostly men who reach the top late in their careers. They know they have only a few years to leave their stamp on the company and to win the enormous financial rewards that can go with this. For such officers to worry about what in corporate thinking are regarded as externalities (factors not directly impinging on the bottom line), such as climate change, other forms of environmental degradation and the problem of peak oil, is to be drawn away from their central task. Their mission is to reap profits for the company and dividends for shareholders. Increased profits for such companies are most often realized when productivity is increased and the number of employees is decreased, when lucrative acquisitions of other companies are made, and when nonproductive operations of the company are shut down or sold off.

Departing from this focus and these priorities is highly undesirable in this corporate culture. Intensifying what these companies do is what is valued in an executive. Blue sky explorations of extraneous matters like climate change would tend to subtract from rather than add to an executive's résumé.

The same things tend to be true of the leading members of political parties that form governments in the industrialized countries. They too reach the peak of their careers in middle age and preside over the affairs of their countries for a few years. The time horizon of political leaders, as is the case for business executives, tends to be a short one. Governments have to be reelected every four or five years. Plans that extend much beyond that, although they are regularly promulgated (as in the case of national governments setting targets for reductions of greenhouse gas emissions for the year 2050), mean relatively little. Governments or would-be governments do not like the idea of antagonizing important constituencies by focusing on the need to make expensive adjustments to cope with problems whose effects will only be felt in the mid- to long-term future.

For mainstream political parties, it runs against the grain to propose tough new emission standards for vehicles, and sharp and costly reductions in greenhouse gas emissions for industry. Programs that threaten a fall in profits, a loss of jobs, or higher taxes to pay for environmental measures are adopted only when great public pressure is brought to bear on governments. Politicians who are worried about winning or holding on to office next year or the year after are not much motivated by crises that will erupt sometime over the horizon.

That is what makes the climate and peak oil challenges so very difficult. Indeed, they are unprecedented in all of human history. It is not that in the past societies have not been faced with climate change and environmental degradation that have had harsh, even catastrophic, consequences. What has been called the "little ice age" of the late Middle Ages, a period when temperatures were lower than they had been before or afterward, has been held responsible for the decline and disappearance of the Viking settlements in Greenland, settlements that flourished for a couple of centuries before dying out. The case of environmental degradation in Easter Island, the tiny mid-Pacific island, several centuries in the past, has been documented. On Easter Island, at the height of its civilization, competing tribes sought trees from the center of the island from which they built fishing boats, and sledges on which to move the giant stone statues they constructed. The consequence of the competition for the small supply of trees was that the islanders harvested them all. With no new supply of wood to build new boats and repair old ones, the inhabitants could no longer travel to their fishing grounds. A catastrophic collapse occurred and the population of Easter Islanders fell from a high of about 10,000 people to several thousand, who lived at a much lower standard than their ancestors had enjoyed.

In his book titled *Collapse*, Jared Diamond analyzes these and other cases of societal collapse. The analogy with the current state of the whole world as it faces the twin crises of climate change and peak oil is a clear one. It is suggestive, but it can only be taken so far. For one thing, the variety and extent of resources in the world is enormously greater than was the case in Greenland or Easter Island. In addition, the capacity of technological society to adapt and to develop new techniques to produce energy and to avert environmental catastrophe must not be discounted.

That said, the unprecedented nature of the challenge should be kept in mind. Never before has the whole world faced a crisis that is the consequence of human activities. To cope with it on a global scale, therefore, presents utterly unique challenges.

The fact that in the leading industrial countries and in the rising economic powers, China and India, the ethic that favors growth is predominant magnifies the problem. The dreadful analogy of the whole world with Easter Island — plunging toward irreversible climate change and peak oil, without taking serious steps to avoid calamity —

is not all that far-fetched. In the case of Easter Island, the salient question was: would the person cutting down the last tree feel the enormity of his or her act? For the world, the parallel question is: who will consume the last barrel of oil?

No serious observer expects that last barrel of oil to be consumed. The question, though, is how the plunge toward calamity can be averted. Given the huge benefits that accrue to those at the helm of both corporations and governments for staying the present course, what is to cause a change of course?

The least invasive answer and the one advanced by those at the helm today, particularly in North America, is that the market system itself is the ideal instrument for making the changes needed. The case they make is that as the supply of petroleum diminishes and demand rises, the price will rise accordingly. As the price rises, scientists, engineers and entrepreneurs will be motivated to innovate. There will be a concerted drive toward greater industrial and transportation efficiency in the use of energy. Vehicles that consume too much fuel will be uneconomic. Similarly, industrial processes that waste energy will be replaced by those that are more efficient. Wasteful practices, for instance, the transport of agricultural produce, such as fruit, vegetables, wheat and beef, from one part of the world to another, will be scaled back in favor of the use of production closer to markets. As energy prices rise, transportation costs will become a greater factor to be considered than at any time in more than a century.

While, at present, it is normal for corporate executives and corporate lawyers to travel extensively for face-to-face meetings as they conduct business, this could change. As oil prices rise, so too will the price of air travel. Business travel could be replaced to a considerable extent through the mounting of virtual conferences through which decision-makers meet in teleconferences and via the Internet.

At the same time as energy savings are realized, new sources of energy will be created. Higher prices will make it economic to produce oil from smaller fields and to enhance the production, through secondary and tertiary methods (with steam injection and other means), to lift oil normally left in the ground when a field is played out. In addition, higher prices will increase the economic viability of oil produced from oil sands, oil shales and from the liquefaction of coal. Since much more potential carbon fuel exists in these forms than in the form of liquid oil, higher prices will open the way to the production of enormous new supplies that can meet global requirements for many decades to come.

The market will encourage the development of alternative forms of energy, adherents of the market solution insist. Some of those sources, such as nuclear energy, are already in wide use. Environmentalists have long argued that nuclear energy poses the risks of catastrophic incidents such as the one at the nuclear facility at Chernobyl in Ukraine in 1986. An explosion killed forty-seven people and released nuclear waste into the air, leading ultimately to a sharp increase in cancer deaths and birth defects in the region, affecting an estimated 9,000 people. In addition to the risk of nuclear accidents, there is the enormous problem of what to do with the nuclear waste produced through the process of generating nuclear energy. Nuclear waste is a contaminant unlike any other ever dealt with by human beings. Waste materials from nuclear plants will remain radioactive, and thus dangerous, for thousands of years. This means that present-day production of nuclear energy will commit countless future generations to the safe disposal of this waste. Moreover, so-called dirty bombs can be fashioned from nuclear waste. Dirty bombs fall short of a nuclear detonation, but they can be used to kill large numbers of people and to contaminate a city for decades. The prospect of such material falling into the hands of terrorists is one that already concerns security agencies in many countries.

Despite the ample problems with nuclear power, the rising price of natural gas (used widely in Europe and in some parts of North America to produce electricity) and concerns about petroleum supply are driving Europeans and North Americans to consider launching new nuclear power facilities.

Beyond nuclear power, projects are underway in many countries to produce fuel from various renewable sources. These biomass (from live forms) fuels are made from trees, grain and even animal manure. Fuel from these sources can be mixed with gasoline to power vehicles. Hydrogen is being used in some jurisdictions as fuel to drive buses.

Other renewable energy sources include windmills, mounted in large numbers on suitable terrain, to generate electric power. For instance, beside the highway from Los Angeles on the outskirts of Palm Springs, a natural wind tunnel is created by the configuration of nearby mountain peaks. The windmills located on this huge site greet drivers with an eerie hum. In many parts of the world, solar panels are used to generate power to heat homes. The city of Toronto has experimented with a program to pump cold water out of Lake Ontario for use as a source of air-conditioning in the summer, a way to replace electric power at peak times. At present some of that peak electricity is produced in greenhouse-gas-emitting coal plants.

Tidal power, in favorable locations such as the Bay of Fundy between Nova Scotia and New Brunswick, has been under consideration for some time. The idea is to generate power from the rush of water back into the sea as the tides go out (the Bay of Fundy has the world's most powerful tides). A large-scale tidal power project has already gone into service along the coast of Brittany in France.

These ideas, dedicated to increasing fuel efficiency and to providing additional energy supplies, are leading to action in response to signals from the market. It should be noted that the market has done a much better job of responding to rising petroleum prices than it has to the problem of climate change. The market is, at best, a responder rather than a path-setter in confronting the challenges. That is because market signals, supply and demand, only kick in once a market for a particular product or service has been established. For that reason, genuine innovation, whether in the design of a wholly new product or service, must precede the signals the market recognizes. Genuine innovators, it is true, can be those who anticipate whole new areas where the market can operate in the future — for instance, in the creation of the first personal computers or the fashioning of the Internet — but the market follows from such innovations and then operates to make them more effective, efficient and attractive.

If the market cannot be expected to do the job of responding fully to the challenges of peak oil and climate change, that leaves those who operate in the political sphere and the state as the key actors. The Kyoto environmental accord was drafted by those with this perspective and it was ratified by many important economic powers. The United States, the country with the largest greenhouse gas emissions, failed to ratify the accord. (In part, the US objection to Kyoto was that it did not treat all countries alike. Under the terms of the accord, the developing world's economic giants, China, India and Brazil, were not required to limit their carbon dioxide emissions.) The accord requires industrialized countries to reduce their emissions of greenhouse gases to 5.2 percent below those of 1990 by 2012.

The underlying idea behind the Kyoto accord was that only hard targets endorsed by governments in most of the world's countries would force a change of direction on the critical issue of greenhouse gas emissions. The targets in the accord were flexible and open to criticism because they included a provision that allowed developing countries to sell credits (if they surpassed their own targets) to industrialized countries. In return, by paying cash, rich countries could exceed their emission limits and stay within the bounds of the accord. Despite this limitation, when the Kyoto accord was ratified in February 2005, after seven years of difficult bargaining, it marked a crucial milestone. For the first time, an international treaty recognized and responded to the challenge of global warming.

The growth of environmental consciousness has developed very unevenly from region to region in the world. The countries of the European Union have been markedly more determined to respond to the threat of climate change than the United States. In Europe, adhesion to the accord has been driven by several decades of intense political campaigning on the part of green parties, most importantly in Germany. For its part, Canada ratified Kyoto while the federal Liberals were in power, although the record of the Liberal government in reining in greenhouse gases over a thirteen-year period was abysmal. When the Conservatives won a minority victory in the elections in January 2006, the new government abandoned Canada's Kyoto targets, while not formally withdrawing Canada's ratification of the accord.

In some ways, the Kyoto accord was more significant because it recognized the problem of global warming in a treaty than because of the targets it set. Scientists regard the targets, even if achieved, as leading to a mere slowing of the trajectory toward catastrophe, particularly when the nonparticipation of the US and China is considered. The Kyoto targets represent little more than baby steps toward a solution.

On a more optimistic note, the growth of environmental consciousness in North America and in other parts of the world has made Europe less of a green island unto itself in facing the issue. Particularly, in California, long the leader on environmental issues in the United States, the drive to reduce greenhouse emissions has become a passion that includes a broad spectrum of political opinions. In Quebec, the provincial government has committed itself to meeting Kyoto targets on its soil and the sentiment of Quebecers on the issue has become a major factor to be considered in Canadian federal politics.

As report after report is released on the issue, warning of the consequences of inaction, environmental consciousness grows. Politicians not paying attention face the considerable risk of being shunned by the citizenry if they do not pledge themselves to take action. Taking action, though, is much like changing the course of an enormous ship. The momentum in the direction of catastrophe is very great. As yet, the social and political forces that are countering the headlong plunge into full-scale crisis are not nearly as strong as those that are driving the world along the route toward further economic expansion through the evermore intensive exploitation of fossil fuels.

Never in history have humans faced a turning point

such as this one. On one side there is unprecedented knowledge and the plain fact of a clear-cut warning that we must change course. On the other is the determination of those who hold power in the economic, political, military and cultural spheres, who want to go on clinging to the advantages that chance and talent have bestowed on them.

Oil Timeline

1846 Canadian geologist Dr. Abraham Gesner discovered the technique for refining kerosene from coal.

1848 Oil wells were drilled near Baku, then a part of the Russian Empire and now the capital of the Azerbaijan Republic.

1852 Polish pharmacist Ignacy Lukasiewicz figured out how to distill kerosene from oil.

1858 The first oil well in North America was drilled in Petrolia, Ontario.

1859 An oil well drilled in Titusville, Pennsylvania, ushered in the petroleum age in the US.

1861 A Russian oil refinery was built in Baku and for a short time produced 90 percent of the world's oil.

1870 John D. Rockefeller established the Standard Oil Company as a joint stock venture.

1911 The US Supreme Court ruled that Standard Oil was a combination (a monopoly) that violated the Sherman Anti-Trust Act. The court ruling forced the division of the huge trust into thirty-eight separate companies, many of which were to go on to become major players in the global petroleum industry.

1945 US President Franklin D. Roosevelt met with the king of Saudi Arabia. Since then the United States has regarded the petroleum reserves of the Middle East as a vital security issue for the US.

1953 The US Central Intelligence Agency played a role in the coup d'état that overturned a government in Iran that had decided to nationalize the Iranian petroleum industry.

1960 Under the leadership of Venezuela, the major oil-exporting countries established the Organization of Petroleum Exporting Countries (OPEC).

December 1973 to Spring 1974 The world price of oil quadrupled from $3 a barrel to nearly $12 a barrel.

1979 In the aftermath of the Iranian Revolution, the world price of oil doubled yet again.

1980 The Liberal Canadian government established the National Energy Program (NEP), whose purpose was to achieve 50 percent Canadian ownership of the petroleum industry by 1990. Shortly after being elected in 1984, the subsequent Conservative government eliminated the policy.

1982 to 1986 OPEC lost control of the global price of oil, which sank to below $10 a barrel.

1999 North Sea oil production peaked at 4.5 million barrels a day.

1999 TotalFina, an enterprise that was a merger between a French and a Belgian company, acquired Elf Aquitaine to establish a new giant, TotalFinaElf.

Early twenty-first century Experts agree that sometime in the first decades, the point of "peak oil" will be reached. That is the date by which 50 percent of the world's extractable oil will have been produced.

Spring 2006 The global oil price reached $70 a barrel, and then up from there to the range of $80 a barrel, before it fell back again in September 2006 to about $60 a barrel.

2006 North Sea oil production dropped to 2.9 million barrels a day and is expected to decline further to 2.6 million barrels a day by 2010.

2006 The government of Sweden set the goal of completely phasing out the use of oil in Sweden over the succeeding fifteen years.

2007 World oil price reaches $98 a barrel in November.

Notes

1 The Hydrocarbon Age
1. All references to currency are in US dollars.

2 Petroleum and the Petroleum Industry
1. Michael Klare, *Blood and Oil* (London: Penguin, 2005), 76, 77.
2. Anthony Sampson, *The Seven Sisters: The Great Oil Companies and the World They Shaped* (New York: Viking, 1975), 22, 23.
3. Ibid., 24.
4. Samuel Eliot Morison and Henry Steele Commager, *The Growth of the American Republic* (New York: Oxford University Press, 1962), vol. 2, 207.
5. Samuel Eliot Morison and Henry Steele Commager, *The Growth of the American Republic* (New York: Oxford University Press, 1962), vol. 2, 221.
6. Ibid.
7. Sampson, *The Seven Sisters*, 33.
8. Ibid., 34, 35.
9. Ibid., 36, 37.
10. Ibid., 39, 40.
11. Ibid., 40, 41.
12. Ibid., 44–49.
13. Ibid., 55.

3 Petroleum and Power Politics in the Middle East
1. Klare, *Blood and Oil*, 30, 31.
2. Ibid., 33.
3. Ibid., 34.
4. Ibid., 36, 37.
5. Ibid., 37, 76.
6. Ibid., 39, 40.
7. "Remarks by Secretary of State Madeleine K. Albright on

American-Iranian Relations," March 17, 2000, Washington, DC, Office of the Spokesman, US Department of State. Available at www.parstimes.com/history/albright_speech.html.

8. Klare, *Blood and Oil*, 41.

9. Ibid., 43, 44.

10. For a detailed discussion of the oil price revolution, see James Laxer, *Canada's Energy Crisis*: Updated Edition (Toronto: Lorimer, 1974); and James Laxer, *Oil and Gas: Ottawa, the Provinces and the Petroleum Industry* (Toronto: Lorimer, 1983).

11. Laxer, *Oil and Gas*, 34.

12. Ibid., 36.

4 Russian and Caspian Sea Petroleum and Its European Consumers

1. Klare, *Blood and Oil*, 117.

2. Sonia Shah, *Crude: The Story of Oil* (New York: Seven Stories, 2004), 152.

3. Klare, *Blood and Oil*, 19.

5 Oil in the Western Hemisphere

1. Laxer, *Oil and Gas*, 23.

2. Ibid., 69, 70.

3. For a detailed discussion of the historical evolution of Canada's petroleum industry, see Laxer, *Canada's Energy Crisis*; and Laxer, *Oil and Gas*.

4. Klare, *Blood and Oil*, 60.

5. Sampson, *The Seven Sisters*, 84, 85.

6. Ibid., 109.

7. Ibid., 109.

6 Peak Oil and Global Warming

1. Shelley Tanaka, *Climate Change* (Toronto: Groundwood / Anansi, 2006), 19.

2. Ibid., 67.

7 Unprecedented Challenges

1. George Monbiot demonstrates that the majority of individuals and groups making the "junk science" charge about climate change were funded by Exxon. See George Monbiot with Dr. Matthew Prescott, *Heat: How to Stop the Planet from Burning* (Toronto: Doubleday Canada, 2006), 27.

2. Klare, *Blood and Oil*, 60.

For Further Information

Klare, Michael. *Blood and Oil*. London: Penguin, 2005.

Laxer, James. *Canada's Energy Crisis:* Updated Edition. Toronto: Lorimer, 1974.

Laxer, James. *Oil and Gas: Ottawa, the Provinces and the Petroleum Industry*. Toronto: Lorimer, 1983.

Monbiot, George, with Dr. Matthew Prescott. *Heat: How to Stop the Planet from Burning*. Toronto: Doubleday Canada, 2006.

Sampson, Anthony. *The Seven Sisters: The Great Oil Companies and the World They Shaped*. New York: Viking, 1975.

Shah, Sonia. *Crude: The Story of Oil*. New York: Seven Stories, 2004.

Tanaka, Shelley. *Climate Change*. Toronto: Groundwood / Anansi, 2005.

Index